ALCHEMY
IN A
MODERN WOMAN

A Study in the Contrasexual Archetype

Robert Grinnell

Spring Publications, Inc.
Dallas, Texas

Seminar Series 8

First published in Switzerland:
© 1973 by Spring Publications under the Berne Convention.
All rights reserved

Second printing 1989 in the United States of America
Spring Publications, Inc.; P.O. Box 222069;
Dallas, Texas 75222

Cover design, illustration and production by Bharati Bhatia

International distributors:
Spring; Postfach; 8803 Rüschlikon; Switzerland.
Japan Spring Sha, Inc.; 12–10, 2-Chome, Nigawa Takamaru;
Takarazuka 665, Japan.
Element Books Ltd; Longmead Shaftesbury; Dorset SP7 8PL; England.
Astam Books Pty. Ltd.; 27B Llewellyn St.; Balmain, Sydney,
N.S.W. 2041; Australia.
Libros e Imagenes; Apdo. Post 40–085; México D.F. 06140; México.

Library of Congress Cataloging-in-Publication Data

Grinnell, Robert.
Alchemy in a modern woman : a study in the contrasexual archetype
/ Robert Grinnell.
p. cm. — (Seminar series ; 8)
Reprint. Originally published: Zurich : Spring Publications,
1973. (Seminar series ; 8)
Bibliography: p.
Includes index.
ISBN 0-88214-108-2
1. Women—Psychology. 2. Archetype (Psychology) 3. Women's
dreams. 4. Sex in dreams. 5. Sex symbolism. I. Title.
II. Series: Seminar series (Spring Publications, Inc.) ; 8.
HQ1206.G79 1989
155.6'33—dc19   88–38772
                                                            CIP

(Formerly a publication of the Analytical Psychology Club of New York, Inc.)

CONTENTS

PREFATORY NOTE

The present little book contains the substance of five lectures delivered at the Jung Institute in Zurich in the autumn of 1971. It presupposes a certain acquaintance with Jung's alchemical studies: in particular, the *Mysterium Coniunctionis*. It is to be noted that for the purposes of these lectures the personal element and therapeutic aspects have not been considered. Instead, interest has been concentrated on the general and archetypal background of the material presented, which seems to reflect processes at work in the collective psyche. The author would like to take this occasion to thank the students for their attention, patience and stimulating questions.

R. G.

Rome, 1972

CHAPTER I

WOMAN'S PREDICAMENT AND ALCHEMY

In an essay called "Woman in Europe" Jung considered a problem in feminine psychology which has seemed distinctively "modern" and which in its frequency and salient characteristics has, apparently at least, an almost clinical sameness. The problem concerns the woman who has entered as a rival into the masculine professional world and the strains and distortions to which her feminine nature is subjected. Primarily she suffers in her diminished capacity to further psychological relationships. Persons and psychic relatedness are the primary interests of Eros, whereas things and objects form the interests of Logos. In the "modern woman's" psychology, this personal orientation has gone into partial eclipse.

Traditionally, as Jung observes, a woman's place was at the side of a man, and more precisely, on the side where his shadow is deepest: the side that feels and does not want to see. So, the "traditional woman" keeps her ego in the background and invites the man to realize his intentions in regard to her person. Her own intentions she realizes indirectly through the projections she elicits from the man's anima. Yet, as Jung observes, her own feelings and moods are never naive; they are peculiar to her feminine eros, they do not come directly from the unconscious, and they always contain a secret purpose which is unacknowledged by her consciousness. Thus, even though she connives at the man's illusion that her psychology is like his own, nonetheless her own feminine purposes become differentiated in the relation. Sexuality, institutions, relations in general are subject to this love-relationship. Love comes from within herself as a sort of inner conscience having its roots in her deepest feminine nature, and it is this that holds her in check and gives her secret purposes a scope going beyond unrestrained egoism.

It is precisely this "conscience" that turns negative in the "modern woman." By entering into a masculine world where she is only accidentally feminine, her eros takes on something of the emotional sentimentality of a man's anima, while her unconscious purposes become devastatingly "factual" and power-driven, attaching themselves to objects with positively demonic force. Her affective life loses its personal orientation and its primary activity of relation-building. At this point her feminine conscience imposes accusations and penances on her, couched in the moral language of the masculine intellect, but a language used in a peculiarly strident and misdirected way. "Law" becomes at once the vitiation and remorse of her eros nature.

As is frequently the case, something that is very modern may in fact be very ancient, and the "modern woman" seems no exception. She reflects an indecisive state in which she is torn between allegiances to matriarchal and patriarchal forms of consciousness. She is undecided as to whether she is to play the anima in relation to a masculine mentality or illustrate a dedication to the animus in a feminine world. The result is a sort of shadow-effect in the anima character of her archetypal femininity, where she becomes increasingly overshadowed by the fascination of the animus activities in her contrasexual side.

Mythologically her position is somewhat like that of Athena. In Athena's pre-Olympian aspect she is overshadowed by the guilt of her accidental murder of her comrade Pallas; on the other hand, her Olympian aspect begins in the nervous irritability of Zeus's headache which heralds her birth. The "modern woman" reflects this tension between the accusal of a feminine conscience and the cerebral ponderousness of a paternal mind. In a more positive form, however, Artemis seems to be the goddess who guides her own proper femininity.

The result is that the woman is possessed by her contrasexual side. She is influenced by her unconscious masculinity in a way that is obvious to everyone but herself. She is driven to live in her own psychic background, a world of unconscious assumptions and opinions which continue to realize unconscious intentions but which have smothered her feminine drive to relatedness. Hence the argumentativeness, the "intellectuality" and the insistence on "first principles" which just miss the mark and inject something into a problem that is not really there. This "something" is precisely the shadow of her smothered femininity with its archaic intentions, the shadow of her natural lunar consciousness which has given place to the livid brightness, the *Sol niger*, of her masculine aspect.

Thus she may become a good comrade to a man, but without access to his feelings. And on the other hand, her animus has blocked the approaches to her own feelings. The consequences that can follow from this situation are unfortunate. She may become frigid as a defense against the masculine type of sexuality which corresponds to her masculine type of mind. If this defense is unsuccessful, she develops an aggressive, urgent, spasmodic type of sexuality with perverse undertones which is more like a man's than the receptive sexuality of a woman. Or finally, she may develop a sort of optional homosexuality with herself in the masculine role.

This last may be quite unconscious, or may manifest itself in fantasies which evoke great repugnance in the conscious mind; for she has a tendency to detest women in general and herself in particular for

7

being a woman. It is also to be noted that not only does she often find herself, quite unaware, in association with men of homosexual tendencies, but also a masculine homosexual content in her dreams and fantasies will be detectable along with her lesbian fantasies. She seeks to insert herself into a masculine world by means of an unrecognized masculine type of homoerotic relation. This masculine world then becomes a sort of "male mother" which compensates for her unconscious partnership in the "paternal sorority" of her archaic animus identification.

In its broadest outlines the problem of the "modern woman" seems to fit into what Jung calls the psychology of possession. This consists in the identification of the ego-personality with a complex: that is, with the persona, the shadow, the anima or animus, or even with what would seem to be an ancestral personality. This identification means that a certain fragment of the personality obtains mastery for one reason or another, leading to compulsions, phobias, obsessions, idiosyncracies, or pathologically stubborn manias of "self-affirmation." Depression also belongs to this disturbance. Usually, too, there are vivid fantasies about "what others are thinking or saying" — inevitably discreditable, and springing from the most contemptible motives. Indeed, Jung was unwilling to draw a hard and fast line between possession and paranoia.

It is clear that in the psychology of the "modern woman" possession by the animus plays a notable part, with the typical consequences of an aggressive animus: a susceptibility to second-rate thinking, unrelatedness, a refusal to compare thoughts with feelings, and a tendency to the overpowering moods, depressions, and compulsive entanglements which accompany possession. Moreover, her persona assumes a particularly rigid, opinionated and negative character, and she feels great jealousy in its regard. She identifies with a dominant

8

of collective consciousness which can wear a mask of superior and un-related intellectuality, a virtuous and remarkable concern with "facts" and "realistic efficiency" which accentuates her animus and corrupts her anima character. She finds herself not only stimulating negative anima reactions in her psychic environment, but she herself falls into the pit of unrestrained pride and concupiscence which her shadow has dug for her infatuated ego. Her misfortune is thus not only to con-stellate an anima that compensates for a negative and unilateral mas-culine attitude in her environment, but to personify in her animus identification precisely that conscious masculine attitude which pro-vokes such compensations. The collective nature of this situation appears in the frequency with which its archetypal background tends to concretize itself in "synchronicity" and "transgressive-phenomena" in her environment.

In its most general outlines, therefore, possession shows the follow-ing characteristics: a predominating contrasexuality, a forcible intru-sion of the unconscious, a predominance of the shadow, and a contrasexual consciousness — that is, the exclusion of the conscious-ness specific to a given sex and the predominance of the consciousness appropriate to the opposite sex.

Jung considers this problem within the context of the Sol-Luna symbolism of the alchemists. These two figures taken together symbolize an archetype of consciousness expressing the transforma-tional function of the self. Sol is the symbol of masculine conscious-ness, whereas Luna is the symbol of feminine consciousness. And conversely, Luna is the symbol of the unconscious in a masculine personality, and Sol is the symbol of the unconscious in a feminine personality. The conjunction of these two figures expresses the union of the conscious personality with the unconscious. The ego in these circumstances is a sort of mirror in which the unconscious becomes

9

aware of its own face. It represents a relatively constant personification of the self, and through the "dark body" of the ego, which is the condition of consciousness, there occurs that projection of Sol and Luna which casts the sheen of an archetypal consciousness on the world of objects, and constitutes that field of consciousness which the ego assumes is itself and its own doing, but which more precisely is an archetypal activity transpiring through its own intrinsic darkness.

Ego-consciousness tends to refer everything to itself. Yet it is only one complex among others, and in the alchemical picture Jung views it, as it were, "from outer space." For the ego is paradoxical, in being both the subject and object of its own knowledge, so that in viewing the ego from the standpoint of Sol and Luna as expressions of an archetypal consciousness one sees both its light and its dark sides, somewhat as the earth might appear as viewed from a neighboring planet. Such a view necessarily works a profound modification in the ego's habitual perspectives.

Sol and Luna voyage through the inner world of the unconscious among other figures which may one day be capable of consciousness too. For the psyche contains other luminaries beside the sun; unconscious complexes possess a certain luminosity of their own, giving rise to secondary personalities, and from these the ego can be observed in its dark unconscious aspect.

Sol, as the symbolic bearer of an archetypal masculine consciousness, is a natural phenomenon which becomes human in the figure of the King and cosmogonic in the figure of the archetypal Adam. It thus symbolizes a collective dominant of consciousness with which the ego tends to identify. In the vicissitudes of King Sol one can follow the formation and disintegration of this collective dominant, with corresponding mutations in the ego's experience of itself: its struggles for self-assertion, its defeats and its renunciations. The aging of a psychic dominant appears in this, that it grows old and sterile, assuming stiff and rigid forms which express less and less of the psyche. A sense of incompleteness supervenes with corresponding symptoms typical of a "loss of soul," while compensatory reactions are set in motion bringing into view other luminaries of the psyche.

Luna is one of these luminaries or secondary personalities which makes its appearance when the solar masculine light begins to wane. She personifies the compensating activity of the psyche in relation to an aging solar dominant which is tending toward its dissolution and rebirth. She constitutes a contrasexual consciousness to the solar world, harking back to a more ancient matriarchal world where the sun was "feminine" and the moon was "masculine."

Thus, if the adversary of Sol is his own chthonic feminine nature, his anima, the feminine Luna who dissolves the King in her moisture, so too the adversary of Luna is her own archaic masculine spirit, a sort of black incandescent moon which becomes a *Sol niger* possessing her conscious mind. An eclipse takes place in which both luminaries are overshadowed, and it is in this compounded shadow, in this dark atmosphere of nefarious incest or "*coniunctio*" that the "modern woman's" struggle takes place.

In her unconscious, the "modern woman" is the exponent of this dissolution and rebirth, a dissolution and rebirth that occurs precisely through the animus that possesses her. For if her animus has masculine solar qualities which drive her to insert herself into a masculine world, it also has archaic lunar qualities which work destructively, and so contribute to a profound modification of the conscious dominant. Her "contrasexual consciousness" is by no means exclusively solar; it also has archaic, moody masculine, lunar aspects which contribute to

11

the dissolutions and rebirths that conform to the great rhythms of the archetype of consciousness. So too her feminine nature is not only lunar, but contains within it a vigorous solar aspect which is, as it were, seeking rebirth; and it is this ancient solar aspect, wrapped in the shadow of her lunar nature, that she seeks to realize.

Luna, says Jung, is not only the reflection of a man's femininity but is also the principle of consciousness in a woman's psyche, as Sol is in men. A feminine lunar consciousness is "darker" than a man's; because of its nocturnal quality it is less insistent on differences. This is invaluable for cementing into a unity multifarious relationships, but it also has a lunatic logic that turns a man's solar consciousness into a white heat of frenzy, the more so because it reclines on a bed of unconscious assumptions that are supposed to be "the deeper truth"; it also operates in the dark and can clothe itself in a virginal, seductive "innocence" which appeals to the paternal or professorial in a man. It is only later that a man may perceive that this enchanting "new moon" is more notable for its darkness than its light. Yet, in her fullness Luna tends to cast a soft and mitigating luminosity over things, smoothing out sharp differences and merging things together in a soft and gentle nocturnal world where one can still see in the dark.

But when Luna's masculine side breaks through, her mitigating charm comes to an end. She becomes captious, stubborn, with a brutal shortsightedness that jeopardizes everything essential to her own feminine nature. In eclipse, her consciousness takes on a livid, over-bright hue which puts natural colors to sleep, and her solar unconscious becomes black; it becomes a *Sol niger*, even though her eclipse is seldom total, so that her *Sol niger* may be less black than the *Sol niger* in a masculine psychology.

Her *Sol niger* protests too much that it is "light," because in fact

12

it is dark; she will insist on a great truth because it just misses the mark. She gets to know her *Sol niger* in projection, so that if her eros functions well her sun will not be too dark, and the imago-carrier of the projection may even succeed in producing a useful compensation. But if her eros is out of order, the darkness of her sun will transfer itself to the man who is anima-possessed. He then dispenses inferior spirit for which she will show a spasmodic predilection, while he will surround himself with second-rate women whom he is compelled to over- or under-value. Luna herself will attend to this, precisely at the point where his second-rate spirit becomes less intoxicating than her own.

The dark sun of feminine psychology is connected with the father-imago. Her father is a woman's first carrier of this projection and endows this vital image with substance and form. As logos he is the source of spirit for his daughter, and unfortunately this source may be badly contaminated. If he has "ideals" about women, especially about those who are absent or unattainable, and combines this with a conscious "spiritual" attitude, then the more banal, vulgar, and biological will be his feminine unconscious. Or if he is admittedly coarse-minded about women, then in his unconscious there will be an over-valuation, where his lunar anima chooses to appear as Athena or Sophia or the Virgin. Finally, insofar as he falls into the unpredictable moods and insensate resentments which accompany his infatuations, and finds himself constantly in emotional entanglements which he has "done nothing to provoke," he will overshadow Luna with his own chthonic shadow and will use everything that hatred can do to protect his masculine consciousness.

The daughter is invaded and profoundly modified by these projections and unconscious fantasies. Spirit will masquerade as "intellect," as a sort of monastic "purity," or as a sort of clumsy boy-like "heroic

13

athleticism" over which Artemis presides, but with Athena-like pretensions. She may then finish as Parthenissa, as an august unwedded Wisdom, rejoicing in a special insight into the workings of God's brain which gives her a love for his mind and an admiration for her own. Or she becomes Cassandra, who with an air of direful inspiration reveals truths which everybody knows but which are better left unsaid, and whom everyone dreads for her appalling tactlessness. Or finally, she may exhibit the sort of hectoring and hyperthyroid playfulness of Pallas and Athena, with its unfortunate consequences. Most deeply and most sadly, however, her life resembles that of the Gnostic Sophia, who sinned not by rebelling against the Father as did Lucifer, but in loving him too well; and so she fell from her divine unity and became the manifestation of matter and the world of her remorse.

What the daughter needs is spirit, but the spirit by which man lives, a spirit which does not insist too much or talk too loud, that does not ignore evil nor force identification with evil in collective guise, and which gives her lunar nature a round fullness, a gentle soothing light which smoothes out harsh outlines, awakening imagination and poetry in a man as a landscape on a moon-lit night — a spirit which, especially in the "modern woman," seeks to become a sort of flowing spirit of light which she can pass on to her son.

But if this lunar fullness is reduced by eclipse or by the periodic darkening of the moon in its natural course, there occurs the "*novilunium*." This is a state associated with poison, menstrual blood, basilisk eyes; its light is dangerous to weddings and childbirth, and it produces that "moon-sickness" which comes from Hecate in her rabid canine aspect. Then the whole world is infected, and her darkness becomes the *Sol niger* of her animus possession. The woman is then absorbed into her own chthonic shadow, the sublunar earth with its evils and demonic influences.

This feminine shadow is less clearly defined than in a man; it contains not only a woman's unconscious mind, but also what might well be called her unconscious soul. This "soul" extends into the most hidden recesses of living matter, having the crushing pressures, the congealing coldness, and palpable darkness of the great deeps of the sea. In antiquity this was expressed in the Gnostic image of the serpent, which was correlated to the lower brain and spinal column and psychologically had to do with purely reflex actions. This deep level in femininity has something of the dissociated, hypnotic coldness of a snake, whose sleep consists in coma, without dream activity; waking, it lives on a stored up heat that is not its own.

Paracelsus has left us a most illuminating description of the effect of this poisonous novilunary evil on man's and woman's psychology:

> ...Wherever there is a disheartened and timid man in whom imagination has created a great fear... the moon in heaven aided by her stars is the *corpus* to bring this about. When such a man looks at the moon under the full sway of his imagination, he looks into the *speculum venenosum magnum naturae* [great poisonous mirror of nature], and the sidereal spirit and the *magnes hominis* [magnet of man] will thus be poisoned by the stars and the moon... Through his imagination the timid man has made his eyes basilisk-like, and he infects the mirror, the moon, and the stars, through himself at the start, and later on so that the moon is infected by the imagining man...[1]

Here, a man in a state of depression falls prey to the anima in her negative aspect, and she, working through his imagination, succeeds not only in poisoning his solar consciousness, which becomes a *Sol niger*, but then, possessed by the snake-like unrelated consciousness of his archaic anima, he infects both consciousness (as an archetypal reflective function — that is, the "mirror") and also the luminaries moving in his inner heaven. His archetypal shadow has been activated and has transformed them from light into a sort of satanic "darkness visible."

Similarly, the poisonous negative aspects of a woman's archaic anima character have disastrous effects on the woman herself. Both man and woman are contaminated not only by the projections of their contrasexual consciousness, but also by the archetypal shadow which moves as the active substance in the rays of that consciousness. This appears in the continuation of the above passage:

> Thus the man in turn will be poisoned by this mirror of the moon... and this because... a pregnant woman at the time of menstruation similarly stains and damages the mirror by looking into it. For at such a time she is poisonous and has basilisk's eyes *ex causa menstrui et venenosi sanguinis* [because of the menstrual and poisonous blood] which lies hidden in her body and nowhere more strongly than in her eyes...[2]

Thus, not only is the "body of the man" poisoned by the projections of the poisonous *novilunium* of the feminine, producing sexual dysfunctions in the masculine partner as well as other psychogenic disturbances, but the woman herself is poisoned throughout her inner being, not only in her celestial lunar aspect, but also in the demonic stare reflected back at her from the waters of her chthonic sublunary nature. The whole mirror of consciousness and reflection becomes contaminated by a sort of sterile hotness. She falls victim to the primeval shadow of herself, and this poisons her feminine consciousness, the imago-carrier of her animus; even more, it poisons the divine child in herself which is the expression of her deepest femininity.

Sol and Luna can best be understood as aspects of Mercurius. Mercurius in Jung's view is an absolutely primitive concept, a projection symbolizing the unconscious itself where nothing can be differentiated. He is in effect a symbol of the subjective factor, the unconscious as a dynamic energetic substance correlated with other aspects of energy composing the cosmos. Its essence is symbol-production. The unconscious appears at once as prima materia, as the primal darkness of nature, as chaos, as a radical moisture, as sea, as the container of the conflicting opposites, as the mother of the *lapis*, as the son of the philosophers, and also as the arcane substance: that is to say, as subject, as light, as living spirit, as an active principle that must appear in reality in differentiated form. Hence, Mercurius is at once the cause, the matter, and the product of the alchemical process, at once feminine and masculine, passive and active, the dark background of consciousness, its latent, non-manifest side, from which, as Jung says, consciousness, both ontogenetically and phylogenetically, is born like the day-star, and to which it returns every night. Mercurius is the inchoate source of the conscious complex, the ego, which is the son of darkness and through which the "world" comes into existence.

Alchemy pictures a chaotic original psychic state from which the four elements are differentiated. These elements — fire, air, water and earth — represent the fundamental presentations of the arcane substance, that is, the subjective factor as an energetic component in the universe, co-existing with and correlated to an objective factor constituting the objective world. These elements are psychic elements, or rather, give rise in the psychic sphere to subjective qualities of com-

17

bustibility and dryness, to gaseous and vapor-like qualities symbolized by wind and air, which may be warm and dry, or warm and moist, as the phenomena approach the area controlled by water. Water constitutes the humid, fluid basis of psychic phenomena, tending toward coldness, while earth constitutes the solidity and concreteness of psychic experience. Thus moods can be "vaporous," "combustible," "concrete," and "fluid." Finally, each element contains its opposite in a recessive state, with resonances involving other qualities.

As an example of alchemical elements in a dream, I would like to cite the dream of an epileptic. In the dream he had journeyed to Lourdes to be cured miraculously by the Madonna. But Lourdes, instead of being a *piscina*, turned out to be an enormous dry-dock, and the hotel a giant oil-tanker. The tanker was unusual in that it consisted in two hulls, joined amidships by a cross-work steel binding, as though it were a catamaran. In the bow-compartment of the hold of the starboard hull some mutineers were being reduced. The whole ship had just been painted with red anti-rust paint.

Now, as we can see, Luna in her celestial watery aspect is already present in the person of the Madonna, while the *piscina* suggests the alchemical bath of transformation. On the other hand, the injurious aspects of water are being countered: the dry-dock and the anti-rust paint. Principally, the "container" is receiving treatment. On the other hand, the "dry," fiery, combustible nature of the epilepsy is losing its manifest form; it is in the process of becoming fluid or "watery," i.e., the crude petrolium which the tanker is designed to carry. The double-hulled tanker seems to me to symbolize the brain itself. It is under repair, being protected against the corrosive "rust," the "leprosy" of iron — the metal associated with Mars. Thus, the brain is, as it were, being protected on the one hand against a poisonous dampness, water,

18

sea, fluidity; on the other hand, the heat, the redness of fire has been coagulated into the red paint, which has dried out, solidified, and become protective. Thus a *coniunctio* has occurred between "water" and "fire" in various states of interaction, and *presumably* this has led to the isolation of the mutineers. For the mutineers represent the fiery element in demonic form, the epilepsy, but constellated at a human level. Their position in the starboard bow reflects the EEG findings as a diminishing epileptic disturbance in the right temporal lobe of the brain. The dream gives us a subjective picture of how the psyche views activities going on at a psychoid level of the organism. It correlates the subjective factor active in neurobiological processes with the images of psychic experience.

Thus, the elements and their qualities join together in patterns of behavior, on the one hand biochemical, and on the other, psychological. Moreover, these elements appear in many different forms and at many different levels: at the mineral level, classically in the form of metals; at the animal level; and finally at a cosmic level, that is, astrologically. The connecting links, as far as human experience is concerned, are the pagan gods. For the gods and goddesses are correlated with the planets and represent certain inborn predispositions for characteristic types of fantasy worked out chronometrically in the life of the individual. But the gods are also linked to certain metals and chemicals, as we shall see. Thus Saturn is identified with lead, melancholy, poison; Venus is linked to copper, Sol to gold, Luna to silver, Jupiter to tin.

But Sol is also linked to fire and to sulphur, Luna to sea-water and salt, Mercury to air and quicksilver. As in a horoscope, so too in alchemy, these planetary factors in their mineral and vegetable aspects enter into chemical conjunctions, producing characteristic reactions

19

at various levels of the subjective factor as the vital hidden substance of
the psyche.

Fire works on air and brings forth sulphur. Air works on water and
brings forth Mercurius. Water works on earth and brings forth salt.
Fire is active, worked on by nothing, and earth is passive and works on
nothing. Fire and earth can unite only through Mercurius. Hence,
male and female are produced from three principles: the male emerges
from the sequence fire, air, sulphur; the female from water, earth, salt.
Mercurius is the uniting factor, coming from the union of air and water.
Thus, sulphur and Mercurius produce the male; salt and Mercurius produce the female. Male and female therefore represent the prime opposites, while male, female, and Mercurius, with their inner conjunctions,
produce the Incorruptible One — the *quinta essentia*. The final union
of male and female is the achievement of art and conscious effort, resulting in self-knowledge, in which the active principle is sulphur and
the passive principle is salt.

Psychologically, the alchemical description of the beginning corresponds to a primitive consciousness which is constantly liable to break
up into individual affective processes, to fall apart into four directions.
And since the elements represent the whole physical world, their falling
apart means a dissolution into a purely organic, unconscious state.

In Jung's view, the hierosgamos, the union of consciousness and the
unconscious, carries within itself the mysterious drama of death and
rebirth and the immemorial human emotions which collide in the problem of bringing the feminine and masculine backgrounds of men and
women into harmony with the principle of spirit. This "higher marriage," working at once a dissolution and a creative synthesis, is a mysterious phenomenon for which no psychological explanation can be
given. It is a paradigm, giving rise to a psychological concept which is

20

not derived from the mythologem of the union of opposites. The psychological idea covers the phenomenology of the process, but its nature is by definition inconceivable.

Central to this mystic union is the figure of Mercurius: the cause, medium, material to be united, and also the product of the union. Mercurius is the essence or seminal matter of both men and women: *Mercurius masculinus* and *Mercurius foemineus* are united in and through *Mercurius menstrualis*, which is the divine *aqua*. Mercurius personifies the collective unconscious which surrounds consciousness on all sides and which can be expressed only indirectly through its manifestations. He appears as an original *unus mundus*, as *agnosia*, as a primordial unconscious state of absolute undifferentiation; and yet, as the subjective factor traceable through a whole range of differentiations, he appears in the discriminating consciousness working to recreate again a *unus mundus*, the redeemed world of the shadow. Mercurius is fundamental to the union of the opposites, and without him no combination results.

The ego has a mysterious affinity to Mercurius. The ego, the son of darkness, is the first sunrise: the ego and its field of consciousness is light without and dark within, the *sol et eius umbra*. For in the source of light there is darkness for any amount of projection, and the ego grows out of the darkness of the psyche. Projection is not a conscious phenomenon, and indeed, the empirical consciousness of the ego seems to lack the necessary qualities for projection. Yet it is this projection from the dark body of the ego that constitutes its field of consciousness — a projected sheen of which the ego is unaware, and a natural phenomenon beyond the interference of consciousness. Consciousness in this deeper archetypal sense is itself a projection, having its source in an archetype of consciousness which is projected through the ego and with which the ego tends to identify. In this sense, con-

21

sciousness is a divine instrument, a luminosity not only of the ego but of the self which includes both consciousness and the unconscious, both Sol and Luna in their reciprocal vitality. The ego is the dark center of consciousness, and so, an essential part of the self. In this sense, the ego itself becomes the mysterious arcane substance of the alchemists, and in its sun-like character, intimately connected to God.

Mercurius, in the crude form of *prima materia*, is Original Man disseminated through physical reality; in sublimated form he is Original Man as a reconstructed totality. Mercurius is hermaphroditic, containing both masculine and feminine elements: as feminine, he is both highest and lowest, both Sapientia and matter; as masculine, he is both the Holy Ghost and the Devil.

Mercurius acts as a fountain of renewal in that he symbolizes a continual flow of interest, a sort of vital attention and evocative awareness, moving to and from the unconscious. This flow appears not only in the superhuman divine heights of the psyche, but also in its depths, extending down into "matter": that is to say, down past the deposits of mankind's past experience to those levels of man's fish-like prehuman past, and to the psychoid processes of the sympathetic and parasympathetic nervous systems. Mercurius as the arcane substance is the transforming link throughout. Without his intervention no *solutio*, *separatio* or *extractio* from the fluid, mobile basis of consciousness can take place. Psychic energy remains fixed in archaic habits, and the *succus vitae*, the *aqua permanens*, remains in its dangerous, poisonous, primeval state. For *aqua permanens* is a mode of the arcane substance; its symbol is water or sea-water, an all-pervading essence or *anima mundi*, the innermost and secret *numinosum* in man and the universe, that part of God which formed the quintessence and real substance of *Physis*, at once the highest supercelestial waters of

22

wisdom and the spirit of life pervading inorganic matter.

We can identify various levels between the superhuman and sub-human poles in the psyche, various modifications in the "waters" from which Sol and Luna are born. The water itself, which is the *prima materia* of life and the world in both its supercelestial and darkest material aspects, is a deadly poison and yet also a healing agency, at once destructive and life-giving, insofar as it remains in its primal, untransformed state. It must be "properly cooked," that is, submitted to transformative processes, before it loses its inflationary and disintegrative properties. Between the two farthest extremes, there is a "perceptible water" which produces the sort of crude sun-like consciousness that appears in the primary sensations of infancy and in the later empirical consciousness of the ego. There is also an "imperceptible water" which underlies the "invisible sun of the philosophers" and which gives birth to a reflective consciousness of inner awareness and archetypal perceptions of a spiritual character. And there is the dark water of earthy matter which produces a "sun in the earth," a "central fire" or *ignis gehennalis*, the fiery magma of the core, which is at once the activated darkness of matter and the *umbra solis*. This "water" and "fire" manifest themselves as the active agency in hallucination, in cerebral inflammation, as well as in epilepsy and in psychotic processes. They also move in those storms of instinctual passion which burst forth with the violence of earthquakes from the deepest animal layers of the psyche. Empirical consciousness with its correlated "perceptible water" has its origin in this primitive and dangerous "central fire."

———

As we have seen, Sol and Luna symbolize the opposites in an archetype of consciousness. They are born from the *aqua permanens* as a result of transformations worked by Mercurius as the arcane substance.

And they contain within themselves constituents which are at once their motive forces and their specific *prima materia*. In the alchemical paradigm, sulphur is the active principle in Sol and so symbolizes the motive force in a masculine consciousness, and salt is the symbol for the motive force in a feminine lunar consciousness. Thus we have a sort of symbolic "psychic chemistry" which permits us a certain insight into the nature of possession. It serves to open up the contrasexual consciousness illustrated in the psychology of the "modern woman" and the various transformatory procedures which the "art of the philosophers" sets in motion.

Sol, in alchemy, is not the "outer" sun. Sometimes it is an active substance hidden in gold and extracted as a "red tincture." Or, as a heavenly body, it possesses magically transforming rays. Sol is an active sun-substance, a mysterious power having a generative and transforming effect. As the sun lightens the universe, so in the human body, in the heart, there is a sun-like *arcanum* from which light and warmth stream out. It is first after God as the father and begetter of all things; and the seminal and formal virtue of all things lies hidden in it.

This power is called "sulphur." It is the *prima materia* in Sol, and it has profound affinities with redness and with the sea. The alchemical sulphur is red, hot, and dry, and the alchemical sun and gold are red because of this red sulphur. Furthermore, every alchemist knew that gold owes its red color to the presence of copper (Cu) which he interpreted as Venus, the Cyprian, which is also a transformative substance. Finally, red, heat and dryness are classical qualities of Typhon, the Greek equivalent of Set, the Egyptian god of evil. Hence these qualities of redness, like sulphur, are also connected with the Devil as well as with Venus.

And just as Typhon has his kingdom in the "forbidden sea," so the

Sol centralis has its sea in "crude perceptible water" and the *Sol coelestis* its "subtle imperceptible water." This sea water, sometimes called *"aqua pontica"* and associated with the Red Sea, must be extracted from the sun and moon. Unlike the Typhonian sea, *aqua pontica* has life-giving powers, although, as Jung observes, that does not mean that it is always good. It is equivalent to *Mercurius duplex*, celebrated for his poisonous aspect. This is the Typhonian aspect of the active sun-substance, that is, red sulphur.

The dangerous, fiery nature of the sun is nonetheless profoundly related to water. It results from the "miraculous water," the *aqua permanens* or "divine water," which is a putrefying agent, because, as we have seen, "before it is properly cooked, it is a deadly poison." The divinity in this water is sulphur: it is sometimes called "sulphur water," for *to theion* means "sulphur," and is the same as mercury.

Sulphur is a hot demonic principle of life. In its positive aspect it is a "balm" or "balsam." It drips from the sun and produces golden fruits, wine and gold. In man, balsam is the "radical moisture from the sphere of the supercelestial waters"; it "shines and is a lucent body"; from man's birth it kindles an inner warmth; from it come all motions of will and the principle of all appetition. It is a "vital spirit" having its seat in the brain and its governance in the heart.

In its negative aspect, sulphur has close affinities with the "sun in the earth," the "central fire," the burning magma of the core, called *ignis gehennalis*, the fire of hell. Hence, there is also a *Sol niger*, a "black sun," which corresponds to the *nigredo* or putrefaction, the state of death.

From this it appears that the sun is a *lumen naturae*, a natural luminosity, expressing the masculine, active aspect of Mercurius.

25

Moreover, the sun has a shadow, in the sense that light by its very nature creates shadows, so that in a manner of speaking the light contains and generates shadow as well as light. The problem is to extract this shadow which is emitted by the sun. "The sun and its shadow bring the work of perfection." [3] Sol is most precious; its shadow is most vile. Like all things, the sun bears its opposite within itself.

The sun therefore also contains a black sulphur. This is the dark, saturnine, evil aspect of Mercurius, sometimes called "the Ethiopian." He is the activated darkness of matter, the *umbra solis*, which, as Jung observes, stands in relation to the material prime matter somewhat as the devil to his grandmother.

The sun's diurnal eclipse by the earth, the moon's monthly waxing and waning in its own and in the earth's shadow, and the moon's occasional eclipses of the sun seem to have struck the alchemists forcibly. The recurrence of darkness, of shadow, in all of these phenomena, the accentuation of the nocturnal element of darkness, led them to see darkness as something much more than a *privatio lucis*. For them darkness was a real substance, something which was implicit in light, a substance which must be extracted from light and submitted to transformatory processes.

This is accomplished through fiery red sulphur. The shadow of light is consumed by Sol's redness, by the burning red sulphur which is destructive in its effects. In man, natural sulphur is identical to an elemental fire which is the cause of corruption, and this is kindled "by the invisible sun of the philosophers." This is to say that natural sulphur tends to revert to its first nature, so that the body becomes "sulphurous" and fitted to receive the fire that corrupts man back to his first essence. Sol has a sulphurous light and it corrupts because of the sulphur it contains. Sol is a transformative substance, both *prima materia* and gold tincture, both a *sol terrenus* and a divine Sol who unites with Mercurius as bride in a hierosgamos.

Hence the alchemists say: "From the beginning man was sulphur." [4] Sulphur is a destructive fire kindled by the invisible sun of the philosophers, the gold of the *opus*. As Jung observes, the sun with its sulphur is a sort of physiological component in the human body, or more precisely, a projection of a physiological mythology. The sun is an instrument in the physiological and psychological drama of the return to the *prima materia*: the death that man must undergo if he is to get back to the original condition of simple elements and attain to the incorrupt nature of the pre-worldly paradise. All of these attributes of Sol-sulphur figure as solar resonances in our epileptic's dream.

From this it appears that sulphur is duplex. On the one hand it is a *prima materia* from which the sun is born. As corporeal it is hostile to the *lapis*. It is corrosive, earthy, the "fatness of the earth," and comes from the radical moisture of *prima materia*. It is also called "ash" and *faex*, the inclusive term for the scoria left over from its combustible, fiery, and essentially chthonic nature. It has affinities with images like dragon, snake, lion, eagle, fire, cloud, shadow, fish, stone, unicorn, rhinoceros, hen, water, etc. On the other hand, sulphur also has an occult side, the side which, when purified, becomes the very matter of the *lapis*. Here, it is eminently spiritual. It becomes a "secret sulphur," sometimes green in color, a "male and universal seed," the Holy Spirit, the life-spirit itself. Celestial sulphur is the first and most potent cause of generation. Its substrate is the aetheric moisture and heat of the firmament, and so, of Sol and Luna.

We can now see how, if Sol is the symbol of consciousness, sulphur symbolizes the motive force of consciousness. It is a cosmic principle, distributed throughout the world and in archetypal man. It is the cause

27

of sudden interests and impulses; it acts as the inner energy in a sort of vital attention, a *succus vitae* moving in all levels of the psyche and in the objects of its interests, both in its projections and introjections, in its life as object and its life as subject. For this reason, the arcane substance as sulphur and the vital juice of life is often *not* an authentic content of the unconscious. Rather, it reflects the attitude of a non-personal consciousness in relation to such a content and points towards it. One can follow the activity of this *succus vitae*, this arcane substance, in the gradual formation of phobias, obsessions, perversions, hypochondriac symptoms, and the like.

And here, too, we can see how red sulphur becomes the active principle in compulsion. For compulsion is "sulphur"; it exhibits red sulphur as an unconscious dynamism, as a motive force in consciousness which thwarts conscious reason and will by an inner inflammable element which appears at once as a consuming fire and as a soothing and life-giving warmth.

The efficient and final cause of this lack of freedom, as Jung continues, lies in the unconscious, on the one hand in the shadow, in the secret inferiority, and on the other, in the pre-existing wholeness, the image of Anthropos, which of necessity is only partly conscious. The splitting in man which results from consciousness and its dominant ideas gives rise to the sun and its red sulphur as the symbol of consciousness and to the *umbra solis* as the shadow cast by consciousness. Compulsion has its origin in this tension between Shadow and Anthropos, so that sulphur has a paradoxical nature: on the one hand working as a corrupter and having affinities with the devil, and on the other as a "balsam," where it appears as a parallel to Christ.

At this point another aspect of sulphur comes to the fore, which leads us to the feminine side of the arcane substance. For sulphur is

28

a "companion of Luna." That is, when Sol and Luna are united —
which is to say, when the empirical extraverted consciousness is turned
inward — then sulphur has a "coagulating" rather than a disintegrating
effect. There then appears in the personality a white sulphur, a sort of
cool reflective energy in consciousness which is an active principle in
the moon. Sulphur's specific power is greater in the red variety; yet in
its white lunar aspect it leads to the *albedo* which is the goal of the
moon, just as the *rubedo* is the goal of the sun.

White sulphur consequently introduces the masculine solar consciousness to its contrasexual side. Its "coagulating" effects represent a forcible introversion and reflection which turn the caustic heat of Typhonian sulphur back upon itself and temper the crimson passionateness
and urgency of its Venerean component with cooling "second thoughts."
And on the other hand, as a motive force in feminine lunar consciousness,
white sulphur as a coagulating agency fosters a tendency toward the formation of "concepts," that is to say, reflective ideas which are as it were
the differentiated mental essences of apperceptions, ancient emotional
patterns with their constellating images.

White sulphur accordingly represents a psychic energy leading toward
wisdom, toward a union of thought and feeling, and toward the union
of the highly valued ideas of consciousness with their archetypal context.

This appears in the alchemical picture of the psychology of Luna, in
which salt plays a central role. For Luna, as the feminine aspect of the
arcane substance, maintains a closer relation to her *prima materia*, the
sea, than does Sol; and salt is as it were the crystalline essence which
floats in solution in her watery origins. Hence Luna, the mother of all
things, who murders the sun in her moisture, possesses also the healing
elixir of life, the wisdom of *aqua permanens*. Thus water and the sea
become symbols of the feminine transformative substance. Here we

find the Luna component in our epileptic dream.

As we have seen, the transformative substance has Venerean aspects, and also a Typhonian quality which is sulphuric, caustic, red, dissolvent, and destructive; and yet it has its own inner spirit and its own wisdom, which brings forth new combinations of the opposites from Luna's fluid origins, leading to clarity and differentiation. As Jung says, often this transformative spirit is symbolized by Agathodaimon, a snake-like fertility demon representing a divine germ of unity latent in chaos, working toward wholeness. He is at once moist and dry, cold and fiery, "burning in water, washing in fire," drying out the "radical moisture" and the "fatty earth" of the *materia prima*.

Here, salt becomes the fundamental principle in our psychic chemistry. It plays the same role in lunar symbolism as does its opposite, red sulphur, in that of Sol. Sal is feminine and lunar and related to light, in contrast to "crude sulphur" which becomes "dark" in lunar psychology. Sal is an aspect of the arcane substance, and is a synonym for *aqua permanens, aqua pontica,* marination, *amaritudo, salsatura,* as well as for tincture, ash, earth-dragon, etc. It is related to the *nigredo,* although its whiteness is usually referred to the *albedo.*

Sal in the alchemical picture is at once moist and burning; as a constituent of *prima materia* in its corrupt initial state as "sea" or *"matrix,"* salt represents an astringent, caustic, burning bitterness. At the beginning, the "salt spirit" — *amaritudo* — is nearly black and evil-smelling, having the stench of graves and moral darkness; it belongs to the corruptible body, whereas fire pertains to the spiritual body. Hence the *nigredo* aspect of salt — sea, abyss, the devil's realm, the unblessed and undifferentiated waters before the Creation, the world of sin, endless time, the world of the dragon, Leviathan, the astringent principle in tears, sadness, and salty blood.

Salt also has its creative aspect. It is allied to eros, is the origin of colors, and so leads to wisdom. The first bitterness of salt brings into play the feeling function and reflection. Thus, the bitterness of disappointment and betrayal can give the impulse to a brutal, lion-like burst of affect, or it can produce a sterile, crystalline, snow-like frigidity. Or, on the other hand it can lead to a modification and adjustment of feeling. Here salt is the opposite of the masculine solar nature, which knows and wants to know nothing of coldness or melancholy or bitter reflection. Yet salt leads to wisdom if feeling is complimented by rational insight. Wisdom, as Jung says, is the comforter and is never violent. The fateful alternative of salt — bitterness and sterility and frigidity — is resolved in the smoothing out of the conflict between thinking and feeling; for where wisdom is, there is no such conflict.

White sulphur in conjunction with salt symbolizes a transformative agency in which passion and pain are lifted out of the level of physiological phenomena and primitive affect and acquire psychic identity as "suffering." In conjunction they lead to the activation of a moral factor, and so, to wisdom. Hence, the conjunction of salt and sulphur becomes the motive force in eros, which finds its most profound expression as a sort of feminine conscience.

It is this wisdom-producing nature of salt that leads to the transformation of the sulphurous Typhonian sea into *aqua pontica*. For whereas sea water in general signifies *tincture, venenum,* and *pharmakon,* and where, as we have seen, the sulphur water of Typhon was linked at once to the devil and red Venus, the *aqua pontica* of the Red Sea signifies a passage, a *transitus*, which means healing and baptism. As Jung views it, the crossing of the Red Sea means the crossing of the waters of corruption, of Chronos; and the "other side" of the Red Sea means the "other side" of creation and the arrival in a desert where spiritual

31

regeneration can take place. The waters of the Red Sea are waters of death for those who are "unconscious" and waters of baptism and re-birth for those who are "conscious" – conscious, that is, of the shadow and the inferior functions. Thus, in the psychology of the "modern woman" the wisdom which the salt of the Red Sea produces is this: a cleansing of the shadow with its compulsive Venerean and devilish animus aspects, and a healing of the conflict between a dogmatic solar thinking and the affective violence and sinfulness of passion. Wisdom, says Jung, teaches that the opposite to sin is not law but love; then the destructive powers of the shadow in both feminine and masculine aspects of the psyche are perceived. And so, salt also leads to the desert. For regeneration is a spiritual phenomenon, an *opus contra naturam,* involving both contrasexual worlds; and its locus is not paradise but the desert. In other words, in becoming conscious of one's unconscious, one moves out from the limitation of his time and social stratum; he sees the "gods of salvation" and the "gods of destruction" together. This means that he enters a solitude which is like a desert. Yet only here can he meet the "gods of salvation."

———

Luna represents the feminine aspect of the arcane substance. As we have seen, she is linked to salt, to "white sulphur," to silver, to the *albedo,* the feminine *alba* of the *coniunctio.* She represents the cold, moist, corporeal, receptive but not at all inert feminine principle in the psyche, and appears as sister, mother, and bride of Sol. She is the "vessel" of the sun, receiving and pouring out the powers of heaven, extracting the energy of Sol as a power springing into eternal life. She provides that sense of serene undulating movement, like the moon's path on the night sea, and that gentle and serene and soothing noctur-nal light that enables us to see in the dark, when the sun's power has set. When Luna is at her fullness — at the *plenilunium* — she stands as the nocturnal complement to masculine diurnal consciousness. The "white sulphur" in Luna gives a certain nocturnal phosphorescence and "flowing light" to the aqueous aspect of feminine consciousness, a phosphorescence which contains within itself something of the natural luminosity and ego-character of the unconscious. At the *plenilunium*, whether in the anima of the man or the anima-character of the feminine, the "hydrophobia" of Hecate's "rabid dog" — associated with Luna in her dark aspect — is assuaged. This "fear of water" which can infect the divine child, the self-hatred which can assail the feminine for its aqueous origins, is then dissipated and the "dog" becomes an "eagle" that can look at the sun. Then the *Sol niger*, the "shadow of the sun which is the heat of the moon," [5] is elucidated, and there is an easy passage back and forth between consciousness and the unconscious in both of its contrasexual aspects.

Yet, as we have seen, the shadow-side of light is of profound importance, not only in the daily eclipse of solar consciousness by the shadow of chthonic nature, but also in the rhythmic obtenebration of Luna herself, as well as in the more drastic eclipse of Sol by Luna, when *Sol niger's* livid light remains as a sort of burning corona to blackness. This darkness must be extracted; these eclipses correspond to rhythmic disintegrations of the luminous aspect of the self in shadow. This appears most dramatically in the *coniunctio* of the luminaries, which gives birth to unpleasant results in its early stages.

Luna as *sponsa* to a solar *sponsus* in the hierosgamos becomes notable for her dark side. For she shares not only in the light — in the healing *albedo* of the *plenilunium* — but also in the blackness of the *novilunium*. Here her sinister correspondences emerge. At her fullness she gives a mirror image of the sun as Anthropos, of totality: she

33

becomes the mother where the symbol of totality appears and the hope
of wholeness and redemption; she bears the emergent light of a new Sol
which makes Mother Luna visible. Here she appears as Mother, Luna,
Blessed Virgin, and Sophia. But opposed to this is a dark elenchus of
symbols: ashes, body, sea, white sulphur, salt; also the devouring
black leaden world of Saturn, as well as shadows in the animal world —
snakes, tigers, and most evidently, the baying moon-bitches sacred to
Hecate and Persephone, the bearers of infections of the spleen, of madness, and of epilepsy. Here she is pictured as *nigredo,* as the dark opposite and shadow of the sun. Her kiss is a wounding snake-bite of
death for the sun. Here Sol as both father and son descends into the
dissolution and darkness of the feminine, killed by the poison of the
Mother-beloved.

In Jung's interpretation of the alchemical view, the first progeny of
the *matrimonium luminarum* are sufficiently repulsive: dragon, serpent, sea-crab, scorpion, basilisk, toad — that is, cold-blooded, unrelated reptiles and crustaceans, symbolizing a psychic disposition having
the sharp unwinking stare of a snake. Subsequently, as the process of
transformation continues, there appear warm-blooded predators: lion,
bear, wolf, leopard, dog; and finally birds of prey and ill-omened
scavengers like the eagle, raven, and the vulture.

The evil in the divine parents, Sol and Luna, comes to light in their
children. Sol's shadow appears as the moon, and Luna assumes that
her blackness comes from the sun. Both Sol and Luna are overlaid
by reptilian strata or by animal passions, and only after the shadow
of these monsters has been extracted and transformed, washed in the
supercelestial waters above the firmament, and only after both have
experienced the death of their primeval passions of pride and concupiscence, can Sol and Luna appear in their own forms.

Sol and Luna are primary opposites. Together they form a paradigm for the contrasexual aspects of an archetypal consciousness as the transformative function of the self. As Jung observes, moon-mythology is an object-lesson in feminine psychology. But he also points out that the alchemical paradigm represents almost exclusively a masculine point of view. Hence its judgments are valid only for a masculine psychology.

On the other hand, because of her peculiarly masculine characteristics, this paradigm is of use in opening up the psychology of the "modern woman." In addition, the paradigm does give us a valid insight into feminine psychology if one keeps in mind the relativity of value-judgments in regard to the anima expressed in alchemy, and even more, if one does not lose sight of the way the unconscious is experienced in feminine as distinct from masculine psychology. The problem, as we have suggested, consists in the tension between the anima-character of the archetypal feminine elucidating itself in relation to an impersonal masculine spirit, and the woman as the carrier of the anima projections of a masculine psychology in a masculine world.

This distinction between feminine and masculine ways of experiencing the unconscious can best be seen in the different ways *prima materia* is represented. Whereas in a man's psychology the unconscious as *prima materia* is experienced as chaos, as violent and irrational processes of generation and destruction, in a woman's it appears as a fascinating psychic background for sacred images and rituals expressive of her fundamental feminine conscience. It is here that she finds her deepest significance, the origin and end of her secret purposes, the meaning of herself as the eternal feminine forever bearing the divine child within herself. The feminine consequently maintains a rapport with natural forces and natural symbols which is less notable in a man's psychology, and which, in the psychology of the "modern woman" do

35

take on a character of random destructiveness and egoism, counterbalanced by a peculiar anxious and irritated conscientiousness which has its origins in the accentuated masculine character of her mind.

Nonetheless, as we shall see, the deeper one goes into the unconscious of the "modern woman," and the more the red and black sulphur and the *Sol niger* of her compulsive contrasexual consciousness succeed in dissolving her fixations, the more her relation to the *prima materia* becomes manifest in a characteristically feminine way, but with the peculiarity that her transformational activity does not have a typically anima character, but has a certain bisexual quality which is "mercurial" rather than strictly "feminine." She performs heroic tasks. But these tasks differ from those of a masculine hero in that they have something of the character of ancient ceremonials and rituals rather than raiding expeditions; her voyages are more like seasonal migrations or sacred embassies, processionals outward and return, which become circumambulations illustrating a fundamental circulation of psychic energy. And a secret understanding, a tacit agreement, seems to exist between herself and the various manifestations of *prima materia*, in order that these ritual activities may be accomplished.

This secret agreement constitutes her feminine conscience. It links her to her distinctively feminine background, to her archetypal feminine shadow, and makes *prima materia* for her not chaotic, as it is for a masculine psychology, in spite of the accentuated masculine component in her personality and her structuring tendencies, but rather a world of causally non-consecutive but vitally meaningful ritual activities expressive of her feminine self. There is as it were a certain fundamental "synchronicity" in her relation to nature and in her relation to her feminine psyche. And it is this synchronicity which is the presence of spirit in her archaic feminine world, a spirit manifesting itself not solely as light but in wind-symbols and rhythmic movement, as in the waves in which wind and water meet, and as a sort of immanent luminosity, a liquid phosphorescence, a heatless glowing, as of the sea on a summer's night, which represents a projected reflection of her insight into the darkness of her *prima materia.*

The alchemical paradigm of the conjunction of Sol and Luna and the arcane factors moving in it — the compulsion of the masculine solar "sulphur" in all of its varieties, the bitterness of "salt" as the moving principle in Luna — form the background of the possession which is illustrated in the psychology of the "modern woman." Yet, fundamental to this psychology is Mercurius, the principle of transformation. Mercurius becomes the *spiritus rector* moving in the depths of her mind, aiming at the elucidation of a peculiarly "lunar" spirituality as the motive force of a feminine conscience which would express itself not in the language of moral law typical of a solar consciousness, but in the value-discernments of an eros which are anterior to moral codes of "right" and "wrong." Her true aim is "love" and not "law," and yet her attitude to love has a certain masculine structuring quality which would loosen but not destroy the institutions expressed in the love-relationship, and which would, in a profoundly creative way, free the spirituality of eros from the salaciousness, the depreciations and compulsions with which a merely sexual view of love has surrounded it.

Hence, just as it is Mercurius who is the central transformative factor in her personality and predominates over the transformative activities of her anima character, so too she never loses a certain "masculine allegiance" even in the very depths of her personality. Her feminine conscience, the "synchronicity of spirit" which governs her relation to the *prima materia* of her femininity, the sort of "immanent

37

phosphorescence" of insight, the "flowing light" of her ancient "masculine lunar nature," remains as a fundamental characteristic of her eros. This is fundamental to her individuality and should be respected.

This "phosphorescence" is like a million-year-old consciousness reflecting in the dark waters of her primeval feminine substance. Its "immanence" in the waters means that it is an evidence of the activity of an archetypal consciousness even at the level of a *unio naturalis*; it is an intrinsic combination of nature itself. Functionally, it represents the deepest aspects of introverted sensation.

This intrinsic luminosity is the fluid origin of a primary limiting and structuring factor which reaches eventual human symbolic formulation in the figure of the Father. The "phosphorescence" would thus be the arcane aspect, the fundamental motive energy, of a structuring masculine tendency which becomes the spiritual factor and eventually the *spiritus rector*, moving in feminine conscience itself.

It is within this context that the sexual problems of the modern woman can be interpreted. For the goal to which she is loyal, the unwilled and unconscious purpose which transpires through her frigidity, her impulsive sexuality, and her optional homosexuality, is to realize a spiritual value in eros. Archaic structuring principles are at work, aiming at a *unio mentalis* of a special feminine sort, that is to say, aiming less at a separation from than at a transfiguration of *unio naturalis*, and a freeing of eros from the uniformity of biological processes. Hence, she personifies the erotic reflections of a peculiarly feminine conscience.

Yet it is precisely this feminine conscience which exposes her to her greatest peril, which consists in falling victim to the seduction of the Father's fantasies, so that her loyalty to her special feminine spirit is corrupted. This seduction and her struggle for redemption from

38

this fall appear in her symptomatology: in the intrusion of the unconscious, the accentuation of the shadow, and the contrasexual consciousness, which underlie the sexual difficulties which she experiences. Her
contrasexual consciousness means that the "red sulphur" of Sol has
been accentuated. But this also evokes dissolvent and destructive activities from the unconscious. Her animus forcibly intrudes itself,
producing "rages," violent irrational impulses which have their origin
in the *umbra solis* of her masculine mentality. The Typhonian-Cyprian
aspect of red-sulphur comes to the fore, producing libidinous aggres-
sions followed by sudden catastrophic "black sulphur" depressions,
saturnine and destructive, where sulphur's affinity to the original black
phase of "salt" is most evident. Most deeply of all, *Mercurius menstrualis et seminalis* is activated in his most poisonous aspect.

If she persists in extraverting this red sulphur, she destroys herself
in the ruins of her destroyed relationships. If, on the other hand, she
introverts this energy, she approaches the bitter, salty crossing of the
Red Sea. In such a passage, her animus-possession may be dissolved:
but this means that she must experience death in the desert both within
and outside herself before a rebirth in her animus can occur.

The livid quality of the *Sol niger* which possesses her conscious
mind means that she lives in a sort of chronic state of *novilunium*
that not only overshadows her logos-side, but also deepens the darkness
of her own feminine shadow. Here "salt" becomes predominant, its
original blackness linking up with the "black sulphur" of the saturnine
aspects of her animus. The *succus vitae* of her psyche becomes bitter
and saline, and she is driven more deeply into the shadow-side of Eros.
Here we find the source of her sexual frigidity, her impulsive, aggressive sexuality, and her homosexual unconscious. Eros, with its bitterness, throws her back onto the dark chthonic side of her lunar nature;

the fiery and chilling "basilisk stare and menstrual poison" to which Paracelsus referred is reflected back at her not only from the demonic masculine component that possesses her, but from the very sea which has become the poisonous *prima materia* of herself.

Her first task must be to turn the "red sulphur" in her conscious attitude inward upon herself. She must first "cross the Red Sea" and experience the bath in the *aqua pontica* of "death and resurrection." Next, she must celebrate a sort of totemic "last supper" with her corrupted femininity. Only then can she begin the "sacred embassies" which constitute her heroic task, and through which she redeems and re-establishes relatedness with her own femininity. And finally, she must arrive at the experience of the "cold serpent-spirit" with his wisdom which moves in her feminine nature, and which will aid her in linking the "dark waters" of her feminine depths to the "super-celestial waters" of her feminine spirituality.

The "modern woman" is at once the victim and exponent of two compulsions. On her masculine side she illustrates "sulphur" as "compulsion," as a hot demonic principle of life, at once Typhonian and Venerean, at once destructive and revitalizing, working in the shadow of Anthropos in his masculine aspect as a compulsion having its origin in the solar psychology of the dominant of consciousness. But on the lunar side of her nature, she is the victim and agent of "salt" as the motive energy in a peculiarly feminine form of compulsion, and moreover, salt in its black aspect, as a deathly, frigid, paralyzing agency having its origin in her shadow and in the shadow of the feminine side of the self. Salt drives her with all the power of eros to seek out situations of bitterness, depression, and shattering despair. She is caught between these two agencies, and her way out of this dilemma must be to seek the cooling reflective "white sulphur" principle of consciousness through which sulphuric and saline agencies can be united. This has its perils, for it is "white sulphur" which abets her conniving at the illusion that her mind is like a man's, and so opens the way to a false "*rubedo*" of red sulphur. Yet if this seduction is resisted, if bitterness is digested, then "white sulphur" leads her to the phosphorescent luminosity in her deepest nature, the origin of a peculiar "photo-sensitivity," a special reflective disposition in her personality, which can give rise to insights and wisdom going beyond her contemporary world. She is then "modern" not because she has participated in its ancient bitternesses and contributed indeed to their current astringency, but because morally she turns its attention forward toward a value still partially unknown and in the process of formation.

———

It is important at this point not to confuse the "animosity" which may characterize her behavior in the conscious world with a deeper "masculine" quality which, as we shall see, is not necessarily correlated to biological sexual differences. Empirically, her animus is most pronounced and "negative" at two levels, both of which have primarily to do with her ego and her adaptation to collective consciousness. That is, her symptomatology centers on conflicts between her ego and her experience of the masculine component within herself. Both of these levels can be "integrated," and this integration has primarily to do with her ego-psychology and adaptation — it has primarily to do with therapy.

But, as we shall see, our present interest and the deeper meaning of the phenomena illustrated by the "modern woman" lies at the archetypal level: that is, at a level where the masculine archetype and an archetypal femininity are in conjunction, and where a creative process

41

of extraction of a transformational anima-character is going on. These levels *cannot* be integrated. They constitute archetypal patterns belonging to the collective psyche: they are transpersonal and even trans-psychological; and for this reason they have a cosmogonic and eschatological character. At this level the "psychopathology" belongs to the processions of the aeons; these processions are destinal, collective, and go beyond what is usually called animus or anima. Herein lies the real *pathos* of the modern woman, for she is the carrier of processes which, by their very nature, cannot be integrated, but must be borne. It is to this that her feminine conscience carries her and lends her a dignity far beyond the ego's world of consciousness. This she can only contemplate, and acquiesce in a spirit which, in times past, was recognized as a visitation of God.

CHAPTER II

COMPLEXIO OPPOSITORUM:
THE SITUATION OF CONFLICT

Beginning with the "crossing of the Red Sea," the above motifs
constitute a first stage in the individuation of the "modern woman"
and also the beginning of the first stage in the feminine version of the
mysterium coniunctionis: that is to say, the *unio mentalis* or "separation from the body," after which should follow the reunion of *unio
mentalis* to a "transfigured body," and the final stage, the *unus mundus.*

The following case presents the vicissitudes of a "modern woman"
in experiencing the initial phase of this first stage of the *coniunctio*, the
unio mentalis; it is an "initial phase" in the sense that in the material
which follows certain physiological symptoms which had become acute
were transformed into psychic contents.

For reasons of discretion it has seemed right to suppress all material
of a personal nature emerging in the anamnesis of this case. The dream
material is that of a person whom I have designated by the letter A.
The symptomatology in the case is typical of the "modern woman," and
appears in this case as in many others. So, too, the general nature of
the professional interest and success, the age when symptoms became
acute, the type of family background, the social, political and cultural
orientation are typical. In addition, in these cases there is usually a
diversity of ethnic origins in the parents, which, in Italy, has interesting
consequences. Not only are the dreams of a Venetian quite different

43

from those of a Roman or a Florentine, which in turn differ from each other in characteristic ways, but there are also marked diversities in the ancestral strata of the unconscious of a given province. Sicily is the most notable example in this regard, with its Greek, Norman and Arabian influences, not to mention traces of the Sicilian background that still survive in dreams and in local festas.

The present case is remarkable for the high degree of cultural attainment in the patient's mother, who seems to have been a precursor, as it were, for the problems of women today. Also — something of a rarity in Italy — she seems to have been an introverted feeling type of extraordinary depth and sensitivity. This introverted feeling in the mother probably represented an almost insoluble problem for the daughter in relation to her own femininity, a problem aggravated by her mother's own extremely negative mother complex.

The patient, who is thirty-four years of age, and who has been very successful as a producer in the cinema world, has been subject to severe depressions with suicidal tendencies. In addition she had previously been much addicted to alcohol and drugs, although those habits have now disappeared. Her central problem consists in an excruciating sense of guilt and shame in regard to a sexual relationship. She feels that she has been "possessed" — although intellectually she is convinced of the absurdity of this idea. She has no feeling of sexual participation in erotic encounters, and yet feels impelled to seek them, invariably with men who are "impossible" — either because married or neurotic (often with homosexual aspects). If a "possible" relationship offers, she proceeds to destroy it brutally as soon as sexuality has entered. There then follows the sequence of depression, guilt, shame and self-destructive tendencies. She also has overpowering fits of rage in which her voice alters and becomes masculine. Finally she has homosexual fantasies which are linked with the violent reactions of vomiting and nausea which sexual relations usually occasion. She has suffered at various periods from asthma and sporadic attacks of compulsive eating.

In effect, she is in the grip of a demonic animus-possession: she has been driven by a relentless hatred of femininity, both in herself and in others. This possession violates a great sweetness and generosity of disposition, a genuine feminine charm, and it distorts her really good intelligence. It produces in her those stratified symptoms which we have noted: frigidity, compulsive urgent sexuality and an optional homosexual tendency with herself in the masculine role, which appears in fantasies. Her depression and guilt stem from the collision between the interior, instinctive feminine conscience to which I have referred and a collective masculine dominant of consciousness with which she has identified.

Her childhood prefigured her later conflicts. She was idolized by her father, and in her early girlhood she was very much a "tomboy." Her mother, an extremely beautiful woman, was reserved and puritan, apparently contemptuous of sexuality. She seems to have been emotionally and sexually monogamous rather than frigid in her married life. The patient sided first with the father, then later with the mother and hated her father; she devoted herself to her mother's last years as she was dying of cancer. Her brother, depreciated by her parents, seems to have been pathologically jealous of her, and on two occasions seriously tried to kill her.

Her life has until recently been one of violent "red sulphur" rebellion against everything the family had stood for, a desperate and frustrating search for "freedom" and a "new world" — politically, socially, and artistically — a search which has constantly betrayed her. In her youth, after the war, out of rebellion against the pre-war world of Italy, she like many others identified with the sort of leftist dominant of collective consciousness which is personified in *avant-garde* intellectual, literary and theatrical circles. Along with this, she has tried to conform to the current depreciation of religious, moral and sexual values. This repression and devaluation of the moral factor has obviously damaged her inner self, producing the devasting sense of incompleteness which is characteristic of an aging and sterile collective conscious dominant.

The third meeting with *A* was of great importance, in that all of the fundamental symptoms of her neurosis made their appearance, accompanied by a dream which presented with great clarity the "situation of distress" and *nigredo* which is central to the initial stages of the *coniunctio*. These symptoms fall into three groups. One centers on a spasm of compulsive eating, followed by violent nausea and vomiting — a symptom which seems to be common in women of this type. Secondly, lesbian fantasies appear, occasioning great repugnance and despair, in which she sees an amorously excited man pursuing a young Negro girl; this fantasy terminates with herself becoming that man. And finally, there is the onset of a severe attack of asthma. These symptoms followed on an erotic relation in which, as usual, she felt not only no participation, but rather a sense of deep humiliation and disgust accompanied by nausea and vomiting. In addition, there occured the following dream:

> The scene is Palestine, a desert-landscape, and war games are in course between the local people and the English. At a certain point, by accident, I kill a youth, the son of the chief of the Palestinians. At that moment the war becomes real. I am forced to flee. I go to a bank, but the directress is too busy to see me. In a fit of rage I

go out and arrive at an abandoned house by the sea where
an old servant woman brings me rotted pork or bacon to
eat. Before she does so, however, a hydraulic engineer
takes it and washes it off.

Before considering the various symptoms which became acute at
this time, I would first like to consider briefly the dream which seems
to me to give their underlying meaning. Next, I would like to give a
brief indication of the psychoanalytical view of these symptoms. And
finally, I would like to consider them from the standpoint of the alchemical paradigm of the psychology of possession.

The dream pictures a conflict situation which has not been "taken
seriously." For A, Palestine represents a desert land of hot sun, patriarchal rigidity and determination, moral austerity and dogmatic, moralistic contentiousness. The English, on the other hand, are associated
with a land of damp northern mists, a green island set in a cold, silver
sea, a people having a temperament of sensitive compromise, calm
civility and a certain inner reticence − a land, too, where the Queen
is head of both Church and State. Hence, the conflict, which initially
seems merely game-like, consists in the opposition between a hot,
solar, masculine psychology and a cool, feminine, lunar consciousness.

The *coniunctio* occurs in the "accident." At that point the conflict
becomes "real," with herself as the principle actor. In effect, a "mythological situation" has suddenly condensed into reality, has become "synchronous," in that the "game" has lost its "mythological" character and
become eschatological, putting original beginnings and ultimate final-
ities in both inner and outer world in a state of acute tension.

An unconscious factor, irrational and as it were causally unrelated
to the tension of the opposites, has manifested itself as a sort of endo-

47

psychic synchronicity. This factor takes charge and proceeds to eluci-
date its meaning in the "destinal events" pictured in the remaining
portion of the dream. This synchronicity constitutes a visitation of
spirit, and activates the feminine conscience to which we have referred.
A "latent logos," a *spiritus rector*, has expressed itself in the accident,
producing the *rites de sortie* which accompany the disintegration
latent image of the self.

The first aspect of the disintegration is symbolized in the youth
whom *A* has killed "by accident." This youth, the son of the chief of
the Palestinians, would seem, in his death, to open back onto a more
ancient world, that of the Pallas-Athena "accident": for *"pallas"*
means both "youth" and "maiden." Thus, the Pallas-Athena psychologem with its military and amazonian associations has been activated,
and *A* finds herself possessed by an archaic memory in which she sees
herself as identifying with an atavistic masculine personality which
emerges after the death of the son. In effect, *A* finds herself put into
a situation of "optional homosexuality" as a result of the "accident,"
with herself in the aggressive masculine role.

This archaic memory manifests itself as a regression which appears
in the burst of lion-like rage, a red sulphur explosion of affectivity,
pride and will-to-power as *A* collides with the "modern woman": the
"directress of the bank." The "red sulphur rage" has thus acted like
the arcane substance and for ̃ed her into conflict with the *Sol niger*
of her "modern feminine" self.

The result of this encounter is a continued regression into the
shadow of her feminine self. Here she encounters the old woman and
the spoiled pork or bacon in the empty house on the shore of the sea.
She is approaching her own *prima materia*, and the old woman represents the "flow of interest" of a feminine consciousness pointing toward

an unconscious content, the feminine *prima materia*, "the fatty earth" symbolized by the pork.

We have here an illustration of Jung's observation that the moods and impulses of the feminine always have a secret purpose. For the "impulse" or "accident" which led to the murder of the youth, and the burst of rage in regard to the directress of the bank, now reveal their inner motivation, which consists precisely in the activation of a feminine conscience that carries her, as it were compulsively, to the central content of the dream: the spoiled pork and its purification by the waters released by the hydraulic engineer. The aged servant woman symbolizes this flow of an archaic, instinctual feminine consciousness, which focusses the ego's attention on this primary substance of femininity; she personifies Mercurius in his archaic feminine aspect. This aspect "attracts" another aspect of Mercurius — the hydraulic engineer who regulates the flow of the healing *aqua permanens*.

The pork is a symbol of the greatest interest. The detail that it is bacon, that is to say, that it has been subjected to curing processes involving smoke and salt, indicates that the feminine *prima materia* in its fatty, earthy, chthonic form has already been subjected to the heating and drying transformational procedures which aim at sublimation, freeing it from the corrupting moistness of the "primary waters." Mercurius in his fiery and airy aspect has entered, through "moisture," to achieve a union with "earth." The "salting" represents a specifically feminine active factor, on the one hand leading to "bitterness" and "frigidity," which act as a counterpoise to *A*'s burst of brutal rage, and on the other, stimulating reactions that should lead to the wisdom and insight of the feminine conscience which moves behind the whole scene. Thinking and feeling have been brought into close proximity, in a *coniunctio* pregnant with new possibilities. "Sulphur" and "salt," the "fiery smoke" and "bitter moisture," represent a regressive union of Sol and Luna and give birth to Mercurius.

This development appears in the engineer who purifies the union in the *aqua permanens* of the unconscious. This act of purification gives us some insight into the nature of the corruption which has attacked the pork. For the "red sulphur" of *A*'s rage turns "black," in conjunction with the pork and the salt. A saturnine *nigredo*, the "black sulphur" element in the *Sol niger* of *A*'s animus possession, has joined the black *nigredo* phase of "salt," and this has cast a blighting shadow on the *prima materia* of her femininity. Thus, "salt," "sulphur" and the "pontic water" of the nearby sea have joined together to disintegrate *A*'s corrupted femininity back to its first essence, and so to create a situation which can give birth to wisdom. The cleansing act of the hydraulic engineer consecrates this transformational process in the depths of *A*'s personality.

But here we must look more closely at the rotted pork. The pork is an authentic content of the unconscious only from the point of view of a masculine psychology. Thus, *A*'s initial attitude toward it represents an expression of the "optional homosexuality" appearing in the Pallas-motif. She adopts a "masculine role" in regard to the *prima materia* of femininity, which turns the pork into an "artificially unconscious content" in her personality. This is to say, repressive mechanisms have been activated, belonging less to the ego than to Sol and Luna. They have worked selectively, accentuating the tension between light and dark aspects of the ego as viewed "from outer space."

On the other hand, in feminine psychology the pork is rather the arcane substance, the *succus vitae*, which, as Jung observes, usually points toward an authentic unconscious content and indicates the attitude of consciousness in regard to it. Hence, the "nastiness" and

50

the "corruption" have a dual aspect: on the one hand they reflect the pride, concupiscence, the solar, sulphurous, lion-like raging energy of the infernal "red sulphur" which is the motive force of the masculine consciousness by which the patient is possessed — a sort of *Sol niger* overshadowing the primary substance of her feminine nature; on the other hand, from the standpoint of her feminine nature, the "nastiness" represents the activation of an archaic, profoundly rooted feminine conscience, following on a *coniunctio*. This conscience is outraged at the extraneous corruption of the vital stuff of a peculiarly feminine consciousness. *A* is accordingly contaminated by an attitude which constrains her to view her feminine nature as though it were rotted pork.

Hence, the pork is "unclean" only to those who are unconscious of its transformational power, and it is *sacer* to those who do. The dream pictures a regressive activation of the instinct to wholeness. An "instinct to unholiness" has been constellated, reflecting a religious instinct which manifests itself in terms of food and hunger, and which is more ancient than those regressive forms of the religious instinct where sex and the power-drive make themselves felt.

In its broadest meaning, the dream sets forth a psychologem corresponding to a definite psychic state in feminine psychology: it is a state of indecision as to whether the feminine is to be lived as the anima in a predominantly masculine psychology or as the carrier of an animus-dedication in a predominantly transformative feminine psychology.

It is within this context that I would now like to consider the various symptoms to which I have alluded: the compulsive eating, the vomiting, the homosexual fantasies and the asthma.

From the psychoanalytical point of view, spasms of compulsive eating represent a woman's fight against her sexuality which is per-

51

ceived as a "dirty meal." Periods of depression, characterized by over-eating or drinking and feelings of being fat, untidy, pregnant alternate with "good periods" when one feels slim, elegant, tidy, etc. "Fat" periods correspond to early pubertal feelings before the beginning of menstrual flow, which usually brings relief. Exhibitionistic conflicts are central here — corresponding to the histrionic state of "war games" in our dream — reflecting an oral-sadistic Oedipus complex character-ized by an intense unconscious hatred of the mother and femininity. The "eating" constitutes an act which releases "feminine tension." In *A*'s later dreams, after the compulsive eating had been conquered, the food motif appears always as a ceremonial act of great solemnity, under-lining the archetypal importance of the contents which precede this rite.

The hysterical vomiting, on the other hand, is not directly related to sexual intercourse; rather it is focussed around experiences of pregnancy and childbirth. It reflects a pseudo-pregnancy, and also involves the sexual sensations characteristic of the person of the opposite sex with whom the patient has identified.

In regard to the asthma, psychoanalysis considers it as a conversion symptom expressing a cry of rage and a demand for help directed to the mother. Yet allergic factors also enter in, as well as a special sen-sitivity in the vegetative nervous system. Indeed, some doubt has been expressed as to whether asthma should be considered a conversion symptom at all. Finally, it is to be noted that from the psychoanaly-tical point of view there is no specific unconscious fantasy associated with the disturbance, which reflects a content situated in deep oral-respiratory conflicts.

It has seemed to me that these symptoms, which do in effect group themselves about various biological and physiological aspects of femin-inity, can nevertheless best be considered in terms of our alchemical paradigm. From this point of view their interrelationship in the patient's personality becomes clearer, and the archetypal aspect of our interests in these lectures can be "extracted" from the personalistic aspect of the symptoms.

For example, in regard to the compulsive eating: the "pregnancy feelings," the "dirty meal," the "hatred of femininity and fight with sexuality," the "release of tension through menstrual flow," and the "early pubertal feelings" associated with this symptom seem to me to center primarily on the activity of *"Mercurius menstrualis,"* which is to say, on a transformational activity which is bisexual and more profound than either *"Mercurius masculinus"* or *"Mercurius foemineus."* This *"Mercurius menstrualis"* is active in the spoiled pork, which constitutes the "dirty meal" of "sacred" and "tabooed" food. Resonances strike out from this symbol, which belongs to the "pregnancy diet" in which "Queen Luna" dissolves the old and sterile "King Sol" in a sort of "uterine bath." From the standpoint of the masculine side of the patient, that is, her contrasexual consciousness, this means a *dissolutio* of the King *et eius anima.* Hence, it means the destruction of her iden-tification with a masculine dominant of collective consciousness and also the destruction of herself as an anima condensed into that identifi-cation. Insofar as "early pubertal feelings" enter in, it seems more plausible to regard them symbolically, as referring to a sort of "renewed virginity" in which a new creative and procreative development has been initiated.

This means, therefore, that while the "old king" is being subjected to disintegrative procedures, the patient's feminine lunar side has been reawakened; the *foetus spagyricus* has been conceived, symbolizing the gestation of a new conscious dominant. The vomiting, the "pregnancy" and the "loathsome meal" thus center on the activity of Mercurius in his "seminal" and "menstrual" aspect, working through the pork and the various procedures of "smoking" and "salting" and "corruption" to which it has been submitted. The whole has been projected down into the physiological level of the psyche, so that the body acts out a physiological mythology.

On the other hand, the "sexual sensations of the person of the opposite sex with whom the patient has identified" seem to me, at one level, to allude to the erotic vividness of her contrasexual consciousness. But more deeply, they seem to allude to eros itself as the essence of her femininity, an eros seen, not biologically, but spiritually, as the motive force in her feminine conscience. There thus enters at this point a homoerotic allusion with herself in the masculine role. Her frigidity also is involved here, not so much as a blocking of feminine experience but rather as an allegiance to a high value of eros as distinct from sexual behavior. In other words, it points to *pudor* as an important psychic value.

I would therefore like to consider this matter of *pudor* in somewhat more detail, particularly in its relation to the patient's mother's influence on her, and secondly in relation to its archetypal aspect in her sexuality.

The patient's mother's own extremely reticent and ambivalent attitude toward sexuality cast a deep shadow over *A*'s first experience of the feminine nature of her body. Her mother's only comment, at the beginning of menstruation, was that "sex is a curse visited upon women."

The result was that *A* was absolutely ignorant of anything connected with sexuality until her first marriage at the age of eighteen. The marriage experience in both this and the subsequent occasion produced a violent reaction, frigidity, and separation, along with attempts to seek erotic satisfaction outside marriage. These attempts were invariably disastrous. She felt then, and still does, an excruciating embarrassment in sexual matters, even in regard to the words expressing sexual facts. This latter trait has lessened somewhat over the years, although my own opinion is that this is a conscious pose and that the underlying distaste is as strong as ever.

It seems important to point out here what might be called the positive side of this reticence in sexual matters. *"Pudor"* is not necessarily prudery; it can also be an indication of a hereditary differentiation and delicacy which may no longer be "fashionable" but is nonetheless valid for all that. To over-ride brutally this reticence could be as grave a mistreatment of one's feeling life as prudery is. In her dreams the sex-motif is not at all predominant. Sexuality as such can probably take care of itself, if given the chance, being "honest" when honestly called for. For *pudor* here has the psychological value of "the secret," the recognition of the *numinosum* of eros and its mystery. The existence of a feminine mystery therefore makes itself felt in this *pudor*, and the non-recognition of this mystery produces reactions as violent as those of Artemis surprised while bathing. The patient concentrates into herself all of the personages and animal reactions of the Artemis-Actaeon myth.

The patient's primary problem therefore seems to be one of eros, of psychic relatedness, and not of sexuality as such. Indeed, it is precisely her attempt to concentrate her feminine eros into sexuality that gives it a psychological — but not biological — urgency having masculine undertones. If she can resist the temptation to overload "sex" and her body with problems which do not belong to it, this in itself will be a relief for both, so that the body will not be constrained to "conversional rebellions" and a life saturated with drugs, tranquillizers, barbituates, stimulants, etc.

It seems probable that she will find "sex" through eros, and this can come about only if she can stop fighting the mother in herself; that is to say, if she can resist the temptation to adopt a "heroic" masculine attitude which constrains her on the one hand to short-circuit the problem through a sexual adventure and on the other to futile reactions of guilt and nausea. In effect, her frigidity in regard to sexual matters comes from the high expectations of feminine feelings, from eros, whereas her destructive weakness comes from a misinterpretation of the psychological and moral grounds of those feelings and a typically masculine over-valuation of a physical relationship.

Eros is the spokesman of instinct and frequently speaks a sexual language. Yet often its intent is not biological but psychological, and it is there that its meaning lies. Eros is the spokesman of instinct and sets claims on spirit precisely because a spiritual factor is present in sexuality itself which works toward symbolic transformation, so that eros and sexuality themselves are psychic as well as physiological, and have aims transcendent to "natural" biological causality.

A's frigidity and spasmodic masculine urgency in sexual matters reflect this tension in the demonic animus which possesses her. On the one hand, this animus is a "red sulphuric," lion-like solar agency of pride and will to power, and yet on the other hand, as we shall see, insofar as it is integrated in the form of a positive animus of inner perception, this agency can have "balsam" qualities entering into the cool and redemptive nature of her lunar feminine consciousness.

The problem of femininity is clearly central in *A*'s psychology. It would seem to have had its origin in her earliest infancy, in a deficient experience of the mother, with a correspondingly distorted compensatory constellation of the mother-archetype. In that earliest stage of

56

identification, the mother would seem to constellate the self and the child the ego. There is a sort of "mutual immanence" of mother and child concentrated zonally. But in addition there also seems to be an emergency, non-zonally bound center of the personality which can, in crises, control archetypal constellations. In this stage both mother and infant relive a sort of archetypal experience of pregnancy, birth, and nutritional development. This is probably the substructure of the "hunger" that appears in her compulsive eating and nausea; it is reactivated here as a regressive aspect of the instinct to wholeness.

Traces of this unifying psychic center can be detected already at the twenty-eighth week of pregnancy. As the infant becomes imbedded in the constellated archetype, the mother becomes the self and the child becomes the ego. This stage, as we have observed, seems to have been deficient in both A's and in her mother's development. Hence the survival of oral traits and images which are so noticeable. The compulsive eating, associated with menstruation, and the hysterical vomiting, associated with pregnancy and a contrasexual sexuality, reflect this earlier failure of passage in the constellation of the archetypal feminine. In addition, it hints at the irruption and disintegration of an archaic masculine ethnic component in the background of the psyche, as appears in A's outbursts of furious rage.

In terms of the formation of A's character, one can also trace the later consequences of this early disturbance in the first weeks of infancy. The mother-archetype remained in an archaic state, while later the unconscious fantasies of the father led to A's Artemis-like "tomboy" development, with a correlated accentuation of her contrasexual side along with masculine homoerotic elements. She became the favorite son-daughter of her father, and hated her mother, by whom she was rejected, while her brother, rejected by the father and over-protected

57

by the mother, became the object of her jealousy and contempt. This masculine character of "son-daughter" comes out in her dreams with a Gnostic image in the background, as we shall see: "a Son, akin to the Father, but of a different substance."

This state of affairs lasted all through adolescence. It was only twenty-odd years later, when her mother fell ill and was dying of cancer, that *A* took her absent father's place in caring for her and discovered the love for her mother which had been hidden during all of her previous life.

In effect, the non-zonally bound "emergency precursor" for the later ego seems to have undergone a hypertrophied development in *A*'s personality, producing a state of constant apprehension, rebellion, conflict and bi-sexual attitude, which appears also in her relation to her own body as revealed in her physiological symptoms. On the other hand, insofar as this precursor to the ego is introjected, it becomes an inner principle of unity governing the synchronicity of inner and outer constellations of the archetypes. Hence, its activity appears in our present dream as the "logos" latent in the "accident," i.e., as a spontaneous, irrational manifestation of spirit. This means that it is here that we can find the activity of *Mercurius seminalis et menstrualis.*

This problem of sexuality brings us to the third factor in the patient's sexual psychology: that of homoeroticism. Here again, the sexual language does not necessarily mean "sex," even though sexual associations and sensations are experienced in such fantasies. Frequently such sexual sensations and images mean instead the vividness of eros, the psychic intensity surrounding, like a bright cloud of sensibility, the communion with a feminine nature which has remained in the shadow of a solar consciousness.

These fantasies – they appear only rarely, and only recently as dreams – began about the age of eleven. Their symbolic intent is clear from the fact that they have never been concretized nor even felt as an attractive possibility, and also because in her girlhood they always took a mythological, fairy-story form, in which she was a princess in a golden coach and loved by a mother-goddess of great beauty. Later these fantasies became more direct and overtly sexual, while her own position in them became very ambiguous and unclear. The only time she felt a conscious interest of a homoerotic nature was on the boat returning from Ischia, at about eighteen years of age, from her wedding trip. A young woman, dark, extremely beautiful and exactly like her mother in her youth, but "softer," was standing in the bow of the ship with the wind ruffling her hair and moulding her dress to her body. *A* felt a profound and mysterious attraction emanating from her.

Also, on a trip in Africa she was deeply impressed by the nobility of carriage, the tall dignity and grace of those women in Somalia who are descended from the original Lybian and Ethiopian elements in the population. These women still wear the goat-skin *aegis*; they refer back to the pre-Greek matriarchal world of Pallas and the Amazon "moon women," where the sun was "feminine" and the moon was "masculine." Psychologically, this world symbolizes a state anterior to the differentiation of a specifically masculine consciousness, so that the "anima character" of the feminine expressed itself primarily as a function of feminine psychology, without reference to a differentiated masculine psychology in terms of which we are now accustomed to consider the anima. The masculine element was still uroboric, an impersonal "wind-spirit." It is a mental stage of development not only anterior to the creation of Eve, but anterior to Adam himself. In the alchemical tradition this passage toward the differentiation of the masculine component appears in the figure of the "black Shulamite" who brings to birth the "old Adam"; it corresponds to the "first transformation" in which the Shulamite appears as a "personality" out of *unio naturalis*.

As we shall see, the figure of the "dark woman" plays an important part in *A*'s dreams and also in her lesbian fantasies. These dark Mediterranean figures are in sharp contrast to *A*'s own blond appearance, which reflects the northern, non-Mediterranean Alpine origins of her father's family. Indeed, in Santa Croce (in the Italian Tyrol), the ancestral home of her father's family, there are traces of an ancient matriarchal world (with which her paternal grandmother identified in a most negative manner) which still collides with the "berserker" mentality of the masculine Wotan myth, a myth which, in Jung's opinion, reflects a pre-Chronos constellation and disintegration of the masculine archetype.

These considerations – the polarity between a blond "northern" and a dark "Mediterranean" aspect of a matriarchal consciousness, the presence of a "berserker"element in *A*'s psychology (as evidenced by her overpowering seizures of rage), and the ambiguity in her experience of the anima character of her femininity – raise certain problems as to the nature of the "possession" present in her psychology, as well as the meaning of the homoerotic element.

In the first place, her possession is not that of a typical animus-complex. This animus-possession seems to be limited to her rebellious identification with a collective dominant of consciousness. More profoundly, she seems to be possessed by an archaic ancestral feminine personality, a negative archaic matriarchal figure – symbolized by "the grandmother" – into which masculine attributes have been condensed. There is therefore a contamination of an archaic matriarchal shadow and animus, against which another aspect of the animus – a "berserker" masculine component – carries on an atavistic struggle.

The homoerotic element enters at this point. Her whole effort, as appears in her dreams, is to liberate her mother's image from the dark shadow which obtenebrates it. Like a hero releasing the enchanted princess, A seeks to redeem her mother from possession by this archaic archetypal shadow, and in so doing, in liberating the anima aspect of her experience of her mother, she seeks to liberate her own anima character from possession by the archaic Mothers. This bisexual role of the "liberating hero" and of an "emergent anima character" is set against the archaic backdrop of a matriarchal consciousness in conflict with the masculine modern world in which she has lived professionally. Hence, along with the feminine homosexuality of her fantasies, there is, as we have noted, an under-current of masculine homosexuality, in which she seeks to relate as a youth among men.

Thus, insofar as the "sexual sensations of the person of the opposite sex" enter in, they represent a peculiar aspect of the psychology of possession in the "modern woman." This consists in a juxtaposition of masculine and feminine homoerotic contents.

The masculine homoerotic union reflects a specific form of *coniunctio* in which Sol unites with Mercurius as "bride." Sol is at once father and son of Mercurius: the sun corresponds to the diurnal, conscious side of the psyche, while Mercurius appears in his feminine aspect, as the mother-bride who gives birth to and is fertilized by the ego-son. Thus a *coniunctio* takes place between Sol and a Luna who has assumed the guise of Mercurius – hence the "masculine" quality permeating the *coniunctio*. Yet, in the present circumstances, this *connubium* takes on a special character. The animus-possession results in an accentuation of the masculine aspect of Mercurius in A's

61

conscious attitude, so that a masculine homoeroticism permeates the *coniunctio* with "red sulphur" contents, while the "white lunar sulphur" appears as a "feminine consciousness" in a masculine psychology.

On the other hand, in the depths of her femininity Mercurius is accentuated in his feminine aspect, leading to a feminine homoerotic relation. Here, the animus is personified by a masculine attitude in a feminine world. A mother-daughter relation is established in which *A* as daughter personifies the masculine actor. The result is that while on the side of her conscious behavior she finds herself acting out a masculine homoerotic relation, and so comports herself as a "masculine sister," "bride" and "mother," on the side of the unconscious she finds herself in a world of amazon "moon Women" who constitute a sort of "paternal sorority" in relation to the mother-world. In her conscious world she is feminine outside, but this is merely accidental to the masculine mentality with which she has identified. In her unconscious world she is pictured as masculine, and so becomes the animus which seeks to rejoin the eros moving in her deepest feminine nature.

The consequences of this line of argument are most interesting. This dual homosexuality expresses a tension between matrilineal and patrilineal orientations in an endogamous libido, in which opposing paraphrases of the incest-archetype are expressed. Layard has shown how masculine homosexuality in primitive societies appears in the "double brother" *connubium*. There, it works as a realization of brother-sister endogamous values, as a defense against the mother, and as an initiation into a sort of "male mother" — the society of men. Its aim, in his view, is to nourish a masculine spirituality and the extension and continuity of culture. This "masculine marriage" — like primitive marriage in general — is quite independent of casual sexual encounters. It reflects a state in which detachment from the fascination of the archaic maternal element, the corporeality of the mother, is still incomplete.

It would seem to me that feminine homosexuality — at least insofar as it is confined to fantasy-life — may be considered as expressing the feminine aspect of the "double-brother" marriage. On one level it is indicative of an invasion and seduction by the unconscious incestuous fantasies of the father. Yet, more deeply, it also seems to represent an effort at communion with the archetypal feminine: that is, to experience the anima character of an archetypal femininity which has been overshadowed by a uroboric, masculine "guardian spirit" and by the corporeality of an archaic negative mother. In other words, it is an effort to experience the anima character of the feminine in terms of a masculine spirituality, but a masculinity liberated from paternal associations and from biological sexual qualities. Hence, the "animus factor" which moves in archaic form throughout the patient's experience of the archetypal feminine. This conflict with the corporeality of the archaic Mother is reflected in her symptoms. And sex, here, means "eros," "relatedness," "vividness" or "numinosity," rather than simply sexual behavior.

Thus, if A tries to love her mother as her father did, she is seeking neither "father" nor "mother," but rather the anima character of the feminine which has been overshadowed by a negative unconscious matriarchal system. A sort of "masculine protest" moves in her amazon aspect, but this protest embraces both matriarchal and patriarchal components to the extent that they inhibit the subjective nature of the psyche in both its feminine and masculine aspects — at a "contemporary" level, and as a relation of "equals."

These observations find confirmation in the character and appearance of A's mother. She seems to have been almost pathologically

63

reserved, occupying apartments in the house from which everyone was excluded and speaking customarily in so low a voice as to be almost inaudible. She had no women friends, and indeed had contempt for women in general, including her own daughter. Nonetheless to *A*, her mother's presence seemed to fill her house with a strange and beautiful light.

In regard to sexuality, she was not so much prudish as reserved and contemptuous. She was extremely monogamous rather than frigid. She seems to have been an introverted feeling type — of enormous self-discipline and reserve, with feelings extremely deep, whose contents can only be conjectured — but outwardly she seemed cold. The mother was passionately devoted to her own brother, who resembled her physically so much as to be nearly her twin. He died tragically at the front at Caporetto in the first World War. This left an enduring scar on her personality.

Photographs — one shows her holding a small black dog (which appears in *A*'s dreams) — allow one to see her as an extraordinarily beautiful and elegant woman, dark, with large deep eyes, a typical "anima face." Yet her mouth does not express sweetness. It is not a "hard" mouth, nor is it sensual, but it has a certain wide fullness and faintly swollen look, somewhat like that of an adolescent boy, or as though she had wept a great deal as a child. She gives the impression that, for her, "eros" might resemble that experienced by a very sensitive, idealistic, and "platonically-minded" boy.

This impression is confirmed by her dramatic and literary interests. She was passionately devoted to the *Sonnets* of Shakespeare, to which she constantly returned until she knew them by memory, and of which she wrote an extremely sensitive translation. The masculine homoeroticism which is so remarkable in these sonnets would seem to have touched some deep center of feeling and perhaps reflects a certain iden-tification with her brother in her own experience of her femininity. A certain eternal youthfulness – at once "youth" and "maiden" or "bro-ther" and "sister" – seems to have been constellated in the depths of her introverted feeling, and as in the sonnets, it looks at love and age with a certain youthful lyric and elegiac delicacy. It is this in her mo-ther's nature that *A* has sought to redeem and love.

At this point we can summarize our observations by returning to our dream. The dream gives us a picture of the central images under-lying the various symptoms which we have noted. Like a drama in three acts, it elucidates the psyche's comment on the psychosomatic situation.

The first act is the conflict: a "war game" between "England" and "Palestine." "English" means "north, damp, cool, misty, green" – a mentality in which the tendency toward relatedness and compro-mise and calmness takes a leading role, and where the "king" is "feminine." "Palestine" means "hot, burning, solar, yellow desert – a rigid, moralistic, dogmatic, exclusive, patriarchal tendency." "Game" means "mythological": in the desert, the gods of salvation and des-truction are experienced side by side.

The second act consists in the accidental murder. Here, the "myth" becomes "real," and an eschatological and destinal factor asserts itself. A spirit-logos has intervened, transforming "fantasy" into "reality." The opposition condenses into a sort of "optional homosexuality" in the sense that shadow effects and a contrasexual consciousness collide: on the one hand she finds herself as a "man" in a man's military world, and on the other in a feminine world in which she plays a masculine role.

The third act consists in *A*'s encounter with the feminine. In her "rage" in regard to the directress of the bank, a solar, sulphurous, lion-like complex takes charge. Here we can see the elements of the dual compulsion in *A*'s psychology to which we have alluded. "Sulphur" and "salt" act both in the shadow of the self symbolized by the directress, and in *A*'s shadow.

Mythologically she has identified with the Pallas murdered in the form of the youthful son of the Palestinian "chief." Here all of her hatred of "modern femininity" and feminine energy controlled by the directress of the bank comes to the fore. The choking burst of rage drives her on a regression, and she encounters an archaic femininity in the "rotted pork or bacon," the "unclean food" of femininity, tabooed and corrupted by the "black sulphur" of the patriarchal consciousness with which she has identified. To this aspect of the dream belong the symptoms of compulsive eating and hysterical vomiting, with its associations with contrasexual sensations coming from the possessing animus complex, sensations of pseudo-pregnancy, and the overshadowed vital substance of an archaic feminine consciousness. Here the tension in the anima-character of the archetypal feminine becomes acute, consisting in the opposition between the anima as the personification of a masculine experience of the unconscious, and the anima as a fundamental character of the archetypal feminine. The resolution occurs in the act of purification by a peculiarly feminine form of spirit symbolized by the *aqua permanens* of the unconscious.

The dream illustrates most dramatically the problem facing the "modern woman." Insofar as she tries to identify with a masculine mentality and live in a man's world, she is also living in her own psychic background, in the authentic unconscious of her own femininity, and consequently, also in her own shadow. For this reason, just as she exhibits a contrasexual masculine consciousness, so too her unconscious

66

in certain of its aspects is falsified and obtenebrated, so that she behaves rather like an anima-possessed man. This is to say that she abandons herself to moods and affects — to rages, elations, jealousies, sentimental-isms, depressions and guilt-feelings. Such affective reactions, however, in feminine psychology, as we have seen, do not normally come directly from the unconsious as they do in masculine psychology; rather, they express a fundamental creative quality of a woman's feminine nature, and because they are creative, they are never naive, but contain a secret purpose. This "purpose" is the creative drive of eros; for eros in femi-nine psychology is not at all a sentiment. It is a sort of feminine con-science oriented toward a relatedness going beyond egoistic values, and it is this feminine conscience reaching back into the depths of her an-cestral femininity and forward toward generations yet unborn that holds her ego in check and lifts her out of the fascination with the ten-thousand objects of "here and now."

Because she has blocked the approaches to her feeling, she loses contact with the normative effects of her moods and the feminine conscience which guides them. They fall into a sort of overlapping shadow — both that of her own shadow and that of the man and his anima. The result, as we have seen, is a partially false unconsciousness in which a *Sol niger* sheds a livid light and her own lunar consciousness goes into eclipse. At this point, an archaic negative femininity takes control: she is possessed by the pride and concupiscence of an archaic, impersonally oriented femininity into which a phallic constituent has been condensed. Eros vanishes from the conscious world and with it the check of a feminine conscience. Her purposes become brutally short-sighted, greedy, egoistic, bursting forth in devastating emotion-ridden scenes. And so she is led to precisely that destruction which comes from her conniving at a man's illusion that her psychology is like his own. The rage and the unclean, tabooed food are the symbols of this psychological state. Condensed into this situation we have mania in the foreground and a somber Dionysian dismemberment in the background.

The "damp spirit," the *aqua permanens* of the unconscious which appears at the dream's termination, constitutes in effect a peculiarly feminine consciousness in relation to the *prima materia* of femininity symbolized by the pork, on which it has a purifying effect. Because it is the engineer who releases it, it can be considered as a function of the analyst's anima which works a purifying effect on the anima character of A's femininity, setting it free of super-ego contaminations and masculine identifications much as A seeks to free her mother's image from the shadow of an archaic matriarchal mentality with its savage animosity.

This "moist spirit" brings us to the last of the symptoms to which we have referred — the asthma. A had suffered spasmodically in past years from asthma. With this dream it burst forth after an intermission of nearly two years.

In my own view, the asthma, although outwardly the most noticeably acute symptom in A's psychological crisis, ought to be considered less as a clinical symptom than as having an important symbolic significance which is clearly psychogenic, and more precisely, symbolic of the process of cure in the psychology of possession as expressed in A's own individuality. This appears, first of all, in its behavior and the ease with which it was brought under control. In the meeting under discussion, the asthma had vanished within twenty minutes of our entering into an anamnesis of the character of A's mother. These intermissions, over a period of the next ten days, would last until the night before the next meeting. Gradually, however, an interesting change occurred. The

asthma, within three weeks of its onset, occurred *only* in the first minutes of each analytical meeting, and could be turned on and off almost
at will, as we shifted from negative to positive aspects of the mother
image. By the end of the fourth week it had disappeared altogether.

This tendency of the symptom to concentrate into the analytical
situation — a phenomenon which I have also observed in a case of stam-
mering — seems to be an instance of the "centering" and "concentration" of the symbol, here being carried out at a physiological level.
The disturbance behaves like a split-off complex which becomes its
own battleground; it destroys itself as a physiological reaction pro-
gressively as its symbolic content is elaborated psychologically in
dream images. In this respect, it forms part of the psychology of the
coniunctio and of the *unio mentalis* or withdrawal of projections onto
the body.

From this point of view the asthma has a "mercurial" quality and
transforms itself readily into a whole range of symbols, relieving the
body from the burden of projected psychic contents. The concentration of the asthma into the analytical session is an instance of this
"mercurial" tendency, this affinity for symbol production, and it
moves toward transformation from a somatic phenomenon into a
psychic content.

This "mercurial" aspect of the asthma means that it acts like the
arcane substance or the *aqua permanens* in the alchemistic paradigm
of the *coniunctio*. It is not an authentic content of the unconscious
but illustrates instead the conscious attitude *toward* such a content.
Hence, the absence of a specific fantasy-pattern. In other words, the
asthma symbolizes the arcane substance as a "concentration of interest" in the unconscious — a process that can also be observed in the
development of obsessions, phobias, perversions and hypochondriac

symptoms.

Viewed in this way, the asthma is less a "cry of help and rage directed toward the mother" than a reflection in the physiological psyche of a curative factor, the "moist spirit" and "white sulphur" of a lunar feminine consciousness in a "coagulating" phase, which is combating the hot, dry, solar, masculine consciousness, the "red sulphur," which has possessed the patient. The conflict and strangling has its origin in this tension between two types of consciousness and two types of spirit. The "centering" of the asthma into the analytical session is therefore an instance of a physio-psychic "synchronicity" which in turn, as we have observed, attests to the presence of a spiritual agency, a "latent logos."

This means that a *coniunctio* has occurred. The masculine component, sulphur and Mercury, representing a union of "fire" and "air," has been brought into relation to the "secret sulphur" which has its basis in the "aetheric moisture" of Mercurius' spiritual aspect. Here, Mercurius appears as the "bride of the celestial Sol" in a predominantly "masculine" hierosgamos. Yet it is precisely at this point that Mercurius' feminine aspect becomes accentuated. The union of air and water which produces Mercurius causes resonances in the "water, earth, and salt," which become the central principles in Luna. The result is the activation of Mercurius as Agathodaimon, as "salt-serpent-spirit," which works toward the development of a "white sulphur," with its coagulating effects, an active principle of a reflective consciousness in femininity. A forcible "coagulating introversion" ensues, so that the whole "union" and "conflict" between solar and lunar components in the personality center on the "air-water" union in Mercurius himself and on the "sulphur" and "salt" which move in him.

The asthma is the expression of this central *coniunctio* transpiring in Mercurius himself, while the "masculine solar" and "feminine lunar" components appear as resonances, with their sulphuric and saline motive energies. The asthma accordingly is a symbol of a *coniunctio* transpiring in the form of psychoid processes in the vegetative nervous system; it is centered at that level which in Gnosticism was symbolized by the serpent. It is here that the conflict between the immemorial passions of male and female and the exigencies of spirit has been constellated. Mercurius himself is the motive factor, the *succus vitae*, in the asthma. In this sense, the asthma, like the menstrual disturbance linked to the compulsive eating, and the homosexual motif, is an expression of *Mercurius menstrualis et mercurius seminalis*, and it is here that *Mercurius masculinus* and *Mercurius foemineus*, with their sulphuric, saline, and aqueous and earthy elements, are joined.

Such reactions in the physiological psyche can also be viewed in terms of the psychology of functions. To take the asthma as our example, it should be regarded as a "shadow effect" or "interference" having its origin in opposing tendencies in one of the orientation functions. That is, a predominantly extraverted "masculine" orientation drives the subjective factor into the body which then becomes demonically animated. At that point, a "feminine" introverted "sulphur" factor, having coagulating effects, bursts into open conflict, bringing to bear subjective forces which "strangle" the opposing attitude. In the present case, the functional tension seems to be concentrated in the sensation function: those introverted aspects of the function of reality which are excluded from the dominant extraverted sensation function, with its compulsive relation to objects, assert themselves in the most intimate aspect of reality which we experience — the body. It is as though introverted sensation, as a "million-year-old-consciousness" of a damp, lunar, feminine nature, forces an inner reality upon the extraverted solar consciousness. Hence the conflict. The subjective factor becomes "real" at the physiological level. This corresponds to the transition from a "mythological" war-game to a "real" conflict" in our dream, with the eschatological, destinal consequences to which we have referred.

The repression of the subjective factor therefore has both subjective and objective effects, leading not only to a defective capacity for relatedness and a contrasexual consciousness and accentuation of the shadow, but also to the somatic effects we have noted, and to the synchronicity phenomena in her life, which attest to the activation of her feminine conscience in a projected state.

A "shadow effect" seems to arise from a tension in her dominant sensation function. That is to say, the contents of the function of the real are not exhausted by her ego's exaggeratedly extraverted attitude. There is as it were a "contradictory pole" — a sort of "fifth function" — in which all the introverted aspects of the sensation function are concentrated. These contents are filtered by the fourth function, introverted intuition, and take on the moral coloring and depressional character of introverted intuition; they are also filtered by feeling as the third function. The contents of this "contradictory pole," this "fifth function," correspond to the radically "other" of the unconscious world, or to the "quintessence" or "*anima mundi*" of the alchemists. In *A*'s dreams it is symbolized by "Australia," the "fifth continent," the "down-under, polar-opposite" of *A*'s conscious European world.

This tension between attitudes in the dominant function of the real means that on the one hand, insofar as an extraverted attitude predominates, the object is violated and coarsened and loses its normative function in experience. This corresponds to the loss of the normative effect of her feminine moods. In its turn, the body reacts physi-

72

cally to the repressed subjective meaning of itself as object. And on the other hand, insofar as the subjective aspect of the reality sense is recognized, the physiological symptoms are transformed into psychic images and the integrity of the body as "object" is restored. This union of the subjective factor with the effect of the object — the physiological reactions of the body — gives rise to a new psychic fact, which is precisely the translation of the asthma into the psychic image of the "arcane substance" of *A*'s own feminine consciousness.

In its deepest aspect, this conjunction underlying the asthma represents a process of transformation of *unio naturalis* into a peculiarly feminine *unio mentalis*, that is to say, into *psychic* experience. This transformation is "synchronous": that is, a non-causal but meaningful relation between her psyche and her feminine *prima materia*. This constitutes "spirit" in the feminine, a spirit reaching down into the "cold serpent" depths of the psyche active in the psychoid processes of the sympathetic nervous system.

CHAPTER III

EXTRACTIO SPIRITUS:
"GHOSTS"

We have seen how the state of possession resulting from a negative mother-complex and a strong father-identification has produced a situation of distress characterized by a predominance of the shadow and an accentuated contrasexuality. The conflict centers on the rotting pork, the feminine *prima materia*, and the various procedures — solar and lunar, sulphuric and saline — to which it has been subjected. Resonances from these psychologems have been projected down into the physiological psyche where the body mirrors the subjective situation. These physiological symptoms center on a symbolic situation of "dissolution" and "pregnancy" and find parallels in *A*'s sexual problems: in frigidity, menstrual symptoms, and homosexual fantasies. Central to these phenomena, their active agency is Mercurius — the primary transformational and mediating activity of the psyche: *Mercurius masculinus* and *Mercurius foemineus* center on *Mercurius seminalis et menstrualis*. The constellation of this archetypal activity underlies *pudor*, the numinous mystery of eros. Working in the introverted sensation function, it links the body's life to the life of spirit through the psyche's own life which stands between them. Mercurius as the moving energy of subjective life in the psyche appears also as a non-zonal center of unity in the total personality. The menstrual symbol and the asthma express this deep activity of Mercurius as *aqua divina*.

The problematic situation is symbolized by the conflict in the desert:

the gods of salvation and the gods of destruction appear in a conflict of opposites in the desert of Palestine. The *dénouement* occurs in the abandoned house on the shore of the sea where a purifying *aqua permanens* is constellated.

This situation is elaborated in other dreams. Directly preceding the above dream, there occurred a dream in which *A* appears on a large yacht along with a group of persons of "cafe society." She struggles into an audacious brilliant-red dress, much too tight for her. The yacht enters a narrow channel and stops. People dive overboard for a swim. On a dare, red dress and all, she does the same and is badly burned. The captain takes her to some simple fisher people and cures her wounds with the pulp of a tomato. Here the conflict between "game" and "reality" is prefigured.

The "dare" in this dream has the same meaning as the "accident" in the Palestine dream. It represents a "synchronous" intervention of spirit, the "spark" which ignites the situation. Functionally, it represents the autonomous entry into action of the intuitive function, which precipitates *A*'s immersion in the sea water, the feminine *prima materia*.

The narrow channel represents the concentration of the conflict of opposites in a "bipontic" situation, i.e., "between two shores." The red dress, the color of passion, symbolic of the orgiastic Venus and the "red lion," the "red sulphur" of the "Typhonian Sea" — pride and concupiscence — produces a state of impulsive challenge. The result is the plunge into the *aqua pontica* of the alchemists, the "burning water" of the arcane substance which begins to purge away impurities by producing an accentuated situation of distress. Yet it is the tomato, also red, that works the cure. The "red balsam" of a positive "red sulphur," a positive solar-masculine consciousness, works like a chrism in the environment of the simple fisher folk who stand in a normal and produc-

75

tive relation to the unconscious. Presumably the tomato's "balsam" effect is correlated to a soothing activity in the neuro-vegetative nervous system.

"Red" is the color of the love-goddess, the color of sin, blood, Dionysus; it is a synonym for the *aqua permanens* which brings dead bodies to life. It is associated with the *meretrix* — the arcane substance in its initial chaotic maternal state. The "Mother" is also chaste bride and whore, as well as sister, daughter and matron — meanings that are always combined in the anima archetype. Red, as the color of the *meretrix* and of Great Babylon, harks back to the lion and the dragon. Hence it also refers to a uroboric state in which the mother merges with her own substance, both consuming and impregnating herself. As far as the anima character of feminine psychology is concerned, the mother is in a process of dissolving and renewing herself in the anima daughter.

A process has been set in motion working toward the dissolution of *A*'s fixations, and more precisely, toward the destruction of her identification with the primitive passions and animal reactions moving in the background of a sterile dominant of collective consciousness. A union of solar and lunar aspects of an archetypal consciousness has occurred. Sulphuric Typhonian and Venerean agencies on the one hand, and lunar saline agencies on the other, have joined in initiating a process of reduction to the *prima materia* of *A*'s femininity. This means that the shadow in that femininity must be extracted so that a specifically feminine light and feminine wisdom may emerge. Such a process therefore involves the transformation of the negative overshadowing mother-character of that femininity and its renewal in its anima character, where transformational energies are strongest.

But the anima character of the archetypal feminine cannot become a definite aspect of feminine self-experience without taking into account the contrasexual side of the personality. Hence, as we shall see, the destruction of the father-fixation involves a return to a pre-solar world, to a "proto-animus" state, where one encounters what might be called a primary contrasexual factor in the biological ground-plan of A's character, a sort of immanent "photosensitivity" traceable even in the minutiae of neuro-biological life. As will appear, the discovery of this factor, its liberation from overshadowing solar agencies, is the fundamental aim of the homoerotic tendencies manifesting themselves in A's fantasy life and in the syndromal disturbances of her sexual life. With the constellation of this factor, which we will examine in the last dream of the next chapter, a reversal begins, having "coagulating" effects which amount to a "cosmogony" — the nascent formation of a new consciousness and a new world.

In our present dream the sterile dominant of collective consciousness is symbolized by the "cafe society" companions. Fundamentally, the problem concerns the feeling function and its differentiation, its liberation from underlying primitive emotions of a fire-like, lion-like, infernal red-sulphur rage, as well as from a sort of crystalline, snow-like frigidity as it is encountered in the feeling-indifference of her companions. Hence the "burning bitterness" of the immersion in sea-water. Yet, it is precisely this same red color, in its cool, soothing vegetable aspect, that works like a healing balm in which the positive side of masculine consciousness and feeling brings a sort of wisdom that comforts.

The immersion in the sea and the burning represents a forcible introversion and self-heating, a state of incubation, in which unconscious contents are brooded over and assimilated. Here the relation between "burn" and "balsam" is fundamental, for it is the "red feeling" in its moist earthy aspect that "cures" even as it is assimilated by the wound to which it is related. In this way, feeling becomes an object of conscious discrimination.

It is important that the patient be taken to "dry land," since in the immersion there is danger of a return to chaos. Psychologically this could appear in paranoid schizoid symptoms. On dry land, in an environment positively related to the unconscious, both the "poison" and the "cure" become visible and remain conscious. There should then ensue an "evaporation" and "drying" in which the uroboric serpent is vaporized and becomes spiritual. The being carried ashore means that a sort of weightlessness has ensued, even though a "black" *nigredo* state remains; this weightlessness means that nothing now remains but the content of the projection; the extraneous concretistic adhesions have been burned away.

The dream prepares the way for the battle in the desert of Palestine and the retreat to the shore of a dead sea. There, as we have seen, she encounters the *nigredo* form of the "King," the "uncleanness" of the rotted pork. The King likewise appears in such synonyms as "lion," "boar," "bear," "leopard," "rabid male dog," as well as "red sulphur," "*vitrum*" and "*hyle*." Here the *nigredo* is fundamental. It signifies decay, suffering, death, the torments of hell, sin. It casts a blackness of despair which is not so much "of the ego" as "witnessed by the ego" and into which the ego is compulsively drawn and transformed.

Hence, the red dress is by no means a *rubedo* state in the sense of a culmination of a psychic process. Rather, it has a livid, garish quality and precedes the depression which is symbolized in the Palestine dream; it is also reflected in the various symptoms which we have discussed. The red dress, in effect, has something of the character of a regressive solification by a negative Typhonian animus. It glows like the last embers of the ashes into which the phoenix disintegrates.

The bath in the sea, therefore, means encountering Mercurius as a transforming union of contraries, where the patient "burns in water" and "washes in fire." Here Mercurius appears as an Agathodaimon serpent-spirit; he is a spirit which is both the cause, the *materia* and the product of the dissolvent activity of the sea. The patient is at once cold and moist and hot and dry. This state is prodromal to the appearance of the smoked and salted bacon: that is to say, the feminine *prima materia* in its "fatty earth-aspect" has been "dried out," sublimated by the "red sulphur" of a masculine consciousness. An inner "slimming cure" is in course of realization, evaporating "fat" and "water." The situation foreshadows Mercurius as active in the asthma.

Nonetheless, as we saw, and as appears in subsequent dreams, it is the moist principle, and the sea- and earth-centered aspect of Mercurius which is fundamental to the transformations symbolized in the dreams. The *aqua permanens* in its aqueous form plays a larger part in feminine psychology than it does in the predominately masculine mentality reflected in alchemistic symbolism.

This appears in a later dream in which the patient enters a stream and lifts a stone, under which she finds a baby girl. The child is thus born of water and the *lapis*. In the dream, however, she warms the child but does not dry it. The feminine must not dry out its aqueous maternal component; the child must not be a "dry baby." Similarly, as we shall see presently, the equivalent to the "interplanetary journey" of the alchemical masculine symbolism appears in *A*'s psychology not simply as a visiting of "four continents," which in alchemy reconstructs the four elements of the earthly Adam and prepares for the celestial ascent; instead, *A* finds the *anima mundi* in a journey to Australia — the "fifth continent" at the polar opposite of her world. But it is still earth and water that are fundamental to the reconstruction of her feminine nature.

The Palestine dream was followed by two dreams in which the journey to Australia appeared. (The patient had no special associations in this regard.)

In the first dream, *A* journeys westward, by way of New York, to Australia. There she finds her mother, who possesses a tank containing small sharks and poisonous eels. *A* puts her hand in the tank and is bitten; her hand becomes livid purple. Returning to Rome and stopping in Piazza San Silvestro, where she seeks help, she encounters only a frigid indifference. Then an unknown young Negro helps her.

This same motif of the journey to Australia appears also in the next night's dream. This time she is leaving the ancestral home of Santa Croce — much restored — and going eastward by air to the Red Sea. From there she is to proceed by ship, confronting the same perils of the "Indian Ocean" — the unconscious — as faced the ancient explorers. Chief among these, of which the captain warns her, is a submerged rock shaped like a crab. An unknown blond aristocratic youth from Santa Croce is there and dives into the sea to escape an approaching Mandarin army.

The young Negro and the unknown young man from Santa Croce are reincarnations of the youth whom *A* accidentally murdered. They are the dark and light aspects of the animus. They have presumably been extracted from the "fatty earth" of the bacon and the *velenum* of the first voyage to Australia. They represent stages in the distillation of the "photosensitive" animus factor to which we have referred.

The Negro is "dark outside" but light inside. The other youth is blond outside but dark inside. Together they symbolize at once the

original Adam and the solar hero who initiates his journey under the
sea. As Ethiopian, the Negro is Ham or Cham, the "blackness" of
activated prime matter. He must be washed in the deep sea and dissolved so that his beauty may come out. Imprisoned in darkness, he
is the product of the conjunction of Sol and Luna. In a sense, he
personifies the activated darkness of matter, the sulphur *nigrum*, related to the *Vetula* – the Old Woman – as a masculine demon to an
archaic evil feminine background. He is the masculine, active, saturnine substance of Mercurius, the corruption of the spoiled pork, the
Sol niger of the Old Woman. He symbolizes at once the curse of *A*'s
animus and its cure – the problem of bringing the immemorial emotions and the seething passions of the feminine, and the maternal
background of the masculine animus, into harmony with spirit.

Yet in this dream it seems to me that the Negro youth has more
positive connotations, and indeed, this is an example of how alchemical
interpretations must be modified to fit feminine psychology. First of
all, he is moved by a charitable impulse, and secondly he helps her to
a cure, in quiet opposition to collective consciousness. The scene of
the activity is also significant: San Silvestro is not only a central
piazza of Rome, with the central telephone and postal offices, it is
also associated with the New Year in the Italian calendar. Hence,
communication with the unconscious and renewal are also implied in
the locus of the dream.

Finally, the Negro's youth is important. He gives the impression
of being the masculine equivalent, the twin as it were, of the Black
Shulamite in the alchemical tradition. He has his origin anterior to
the birth of the "old Adam" and the "second transformation" – the
solificatio – of the Shulamite. Indeed he should be regarded as the

"spirit" of the Shulamite, belonging to her first transformation, i. e., to her appearance as a personality. He is the condition for the differentiation of the anima character of the feminine from the mindless corporeality of the archaic Mother. Like the Shulamite, he is dark outside and light inside. But his light consists in warmth of feeling rather than mental illumination; his governance is in the heart rather than in the head. In this respect he is in contrast not only to the "blond intelligence" of the light youth who figures in the next dream, but also to a figure which we shall consider later: an ithyphallic Hermes, called Flowing Light, who is pursuing a primordial feminine figure called Dark Water. Flowing Light represents a "heatless" illumination, a phosphorescence, where sexual desire is "cold," without feeling, serpent-like. The Negro represents a natural warmth of eros, a warmth which has been differentiated into feeling and charity rather than primitive sexual desire.

In the dream, the help which he offers is precisely this; it is the salutary compensation to the cruel and frigid indifference which *A* encounters on her return from "the other" with the poison panacea. Thus, the Negro brings "a dark light" as help, for he is dark only to the ego's consciousness, and he foreshadows a "light" which the ego's darkness "comprehendeth not." For this reason, his "light twin" appears next as a solar hero and plunges into the sea, carrying this gold light of intelligence down into the depths of the unconscious. Together they symbolize the *coincidentia oppositorum* of Light and Dark, and each, in his way, is suspended on Santa Croce — the world of the "grandmothers" — which is the matrix of this tension.

At this point it is interesting to consider the relation of the light and dark youths in terms of the "parallel homoeroticism" to which we referred in the last chapter. In effect, we have a "double brother" relation on the one hand, and a "double sister" relation on the other, consisting precisely in *A*'s ego and the Black Shulamite whom we have detected in the background of the Negro. This quaternity has been extracted from Santa Croce, from the archaic Mother and her animus. Thus a *coniunctio*, a "double brother connubium," is active in the depths of *A*'s psyche, aiming at spiritualization and the illumination of primitive dark passions.

As we shall see presently, this parallel homoeroticism will receive notable development. It would seem to form part of a process in which masculine and feminine components of the psyche are gradually detached from biological and physiological differences in men and women, so that concrete sexual behavior can no longer serve as a way of misunderstanding a social or cultural mission, or evading a genuine psychological relationship. Later, this line of development will terminate in a psychic situation in which *A* appears as a "new son-ship": a son "akin to the Father, but of a different substance."

As the initiation of this new development, the blond youth begins his voyage under the sea, at once avoiding and undermining the on-slaught of the archaic classical army of a masculine "Celestial Dragon-empire," the shadow of the rising sun. He acts as the gold aspect of the *pharmakon*.

———

These dreams give us further elaborations of the nature of the "burning water," the desert and the pork. In addition, they allude specifically to the poison-panacea, the *medicina catholica*, and to the serpent bite. The livid purple of the wounded hand which succeeds the garishness of the red dress, the livid burns, as well as the Red Sea itself, are aspects of the "burning water."

83

Finally, the "weightlessness" to which we have alluded, with its relativity of space and time characteristic of the unconscious, is here developed in terms of the "intercontinental journey" which is a feminine equivalent for the alchemistic motif of the "interplanetary journey," the "journey in four directions," or the motif of "ascent and descent."

The "burning water" and Red Sea raise all of the characteristic psychological associations with salt and sulphur to which we have referred. *Aqua permanens, aqua pontica, ammaritudo* in its saline lunar aspect, point to the "production of colors" — the activation of the feeling function — and to a development of wisdom which heals the conflict with the red sulphur of a masculine solar consciousness. "Salt" heralds the *albedo* of *A*'s lunar consciousness; nonetheless, its negative aspects are also present, the shadow that must be extracted. It pertains to the abyss, the sea, the world of the dragon, the serpent, the leviathan, to tears and sadness. Yet, it is also spiritual: "a damp and fiery-cold spirit of aether, water, and earth, of wind, light, and darkness, glittering like a star." [1] It is allied to the cold side of nature, the snake-like Nous or Agathodaimon. Salt is identical to eros, seeking to transform bitterness, bursts of affect, red sulphurous impulses, into wisdom and insight. A bleaching process is going on, extracting the white aspect of sulphur with its moral illuminations.

Within this context, the Red Sea has a special meaning as distinct from "sea" generally. Like sea water it means tincture, *venenum, pharmakon*, and in the *opus* it becomes "salt" and "blood" and "red." But more specifically, it is *aqua pontica*, signifying healing and baptism, and is associated with the bipontic narrow straits where the continents meet, as in our dream of the red dress.

Hence, at this point it is primarily *Mercurius menstrualis et semin-*

alis, with his "duplicity," who predominates; he appears in the mid-position between the *Mercurius masculinus* of a masculine mind and the *Mercurius foemineus* of the feminine arcane substance. This means that the menstrual associations of *A*'s compulsive eating and the asthma have become central psychological symbols of mercurial transformation. The *novilunium* in feminine psychology, as pictured in our citation from Paracelsus, has become acute, reflecting the activation of a center of vitality which, while involving the essence of her femininity, has resonances striking back to creative energies deeper than sexual differences.

The crossing of the Red Sea is the crossing of the waters of corruption, and on the "other side" one finds the desert where generation is of the spirit rather than of the flesh. The Red Sea, as Jung says, is a "water of death" [2] for those who are unconscious — that is to say, stuck in onesidedness and unenlightened; it is a water of baptism and rebirth and transcendence for those who are "conscious" — those who have experienced the shadow and inferior functions which are purified by the astringent waters of the unconscious, and who raise to consciousness the inner opposites to which their epoch is opposed. But this means that one must admit that "the Other" also exists: that one must experience the "transcendent function," and submit to a continual process in which the rational data of consciousness are set opposite the irrational data of the personal and collective unconscious.

In our present context, this means that although the *opus* is a work *contra naturam* and takes place, not in paradise, but in the desert where the saving and destructive powers collide, yet, the opposite to sin is not "law" but "love." And it is to this wisdom that salt would lead, where its sterility and bitterness bear fruit, and so bring about rebirth.

But such an experience means leaving the ego's world of "here and now" and entering a world of solitude, loneliness and strangeness: a world of "the other," of the psychic non-ego which is, as it were, "outside" — a sort of weightless world and timeless, which primitives sensed as an alien country of the dead. This world is the lengthened shadow of the unconscious objective psyche.

The desolation of "San Silvestro," the crossing of the Red Sea, the immersion in the *aqua pontica*, the conflict between the contraries in the desert of Palestine — the conflict between the Old Law and the New concentrated in the "unclean food" — all center around the meaning of "salt" and reach a climax in the poison-panacea, the bite by the sharks and eels, in the world of the "Other," the "fifth continent." The *aqua pontica*, the *aqua permanens*, the arcane substance of wisdom, truth, knowledge; the purifying water for the pork, the sea-water, the quintessence or *anima mundi* — the innermost secret spirit in man; the sunken rock shaped like a crab in the sea, the *venenum* which is identical to blood and to the *aqua pontica*: these symbols are synonyms for the *serpens hermetis*, for the burning but curative powers of the cold lunar spirit which is also the *prima materia* of a life beyond good and evil, where the opposite to sin is not the "law" of a masculine consciousness but the eros of a primordial feminine conscience. The variety of these symbols and the variety of journeys mean, psychologically, that during the assimilation of the unconscious the personality passes through many transformations, which show it from many different points of view, and are followed by the ever-changing moods, which tend to re-establish their normative function in *A*'s feminine nature. These changes foreshadow a deep transformation that is like a rebirth.

These changes are like the colors to which salt gives birth; they correspond to the four functions, so that the "greeness" and moist

quality of the "English" refer to sensation, reality, instinct. Green is
associated with a more ancient Venus than the Cyprian, and also with
the Holy Spirit; it is the color of life, of creation, procreation and rebirth. It refers to sulphur in its occult aspect, frequently represented
as green, as the *prima materia* of the *lapis*. The redness, as we have
seen, is associated with blood, emotion, feeling, love, as well as with
anger, destruction and berserker blood-drunkenness. After the poison
of the serpent-bite, there appears the irridescent livid purple, having
something deathly about it, the color of the Lord's Passion and ecclesiastical mourning. Thus, the "restoration of Santa Croce" means
the rendering acute of a religious experience of the conflict of contraries. The regimen of Venus in her orgiastic and provocative aspect
leads to passion, death and mourning. And yet this state represents
a promise, like the rainbow after the Flood, that the Tree of Wisdom
will set forth flowers. Blue symbolizes thinking, while yellow, like
the blond youth who dives into the sea, symbolizes intuition and intelligence.

A's dream-journey goes in four directions and involves four continents. She goes "south" to Africa, associated with "fire" — the
fiery "dark continent." She goes north, so that Europe and England
are associated with "earth." Asia, in the East, is associated with "air."
And America, the "new world" of the West, is associated with "water."
Hence, the four continents, the four directions and the four elements
form a sort of quaternity which reflect the four orienting functions.
They also represent the four elements going into the construction
of the cosmogonic Adam, the Anthropos. They meet at the Red Sea,
which is a point of passage and also a juxtaposition of the antagonistic
opposites of the *quaternio*. Australia represents the "fifth Continent,"
the polar "opposite," the "Other." It becomes symbolic of the "quintessence," the fifth element, the One which is born from the Four,

from the intersection of the opposites at Santa Croce.

As the *anima mundi*, therefore, Australia and the poison panacea symbolize that part of God which for the alchemists formed the real substance, the "divine spirit," immanent in Physis and its four elements. It stands to God, says Jung, as the "accrescent soul" does to the divine soul in man.[3] It grows up through the mineral, vegetable and animal kingdoms to man. It pervades all nature, and natural forms are attached to it like appendages. Figuratively this is represented as a squaring of the circle or as a transition from square to circle. This transition is foreshadowed by the ancient symbol for salt: ⬚ . Hence, it alludes to a union of opposites and is an image of wholeness.

The mineral images which have been constellated symbolize a physically dead but spiritually living matter. Hence, the "cold spirit" inhabits this deepest physiological psyche and is symbolized not only as "poison," as an inorganic substance, but also in the serpent-fish which it produces. The union of sharks and eels in the tank is a product of this *anima mundi*.

Psychologically, these symbols point to the fourth function in *A*'s psychology, intuition, and to the "fifth," the "contradictory pole" of the first, which have their seat in the unconscious. In mythology, the fourth function is portrayed as a great animal, as Leviathan, whale, dragon, primaeval serpent, tortoise, as well as by hot-blooded predators like the lion, wolf, dog, leopard, or as ill-omened winged scavengers like the eagle or the raven or the vulture, or in dreams as aerial beings like aggressive bombers or war-planes. In our dream, the rock shaped like a crab alludes to a passage state between the mineral and crustacean stages of the *anima mundi*. In effect, these creatures symbolize a psychic situation of great inner heat, but also coldness, of intense self-incubation and introversion. The activity is centered in the region of the animal

soul in man; it extends downward through a level containing the berserker specters of humanity's past epochs, and thence, as Jung puts it,[4]
down to the animal souls of Pithecanthropos and the hominids; next
to the "psyche" of the cold-blooded saurians, and finally, deepest of
all, to the transcendental mystery and paradox of the sympathetic and
para-sympathetic psychoid processes. It is this level which has been constellated in A's menstrual disturbance and in the asthma, and it is at this
level, too, that the cure begins, as we saw in the balsam quality of the
tomato.

These elements, qualities and symbolic animals are prefigurations
and carriers of the self. The structure of wholeness is present, but
deeply buried in the unconscious. It can always be found if one risks
oneself by attaining the widest and deepest range of consciousness, but
it requires a self-knowledge and reflective attitude that consists in pro-
jecting oneself into the empirical self as it really is, and not into forms,
rituals, games, dares, or into the "self" as we like to think we are. It
requires a limitation of the ego's sovereignty and an experience of the
empirical ego as it really is, with everything it does and everything
that happens to it, that is, as a relatively constant personification of
the self.

This means that a point of view has been established which first
appeared in the "dare" and in the "logos" latent in the "accident"
of the Palestine dream, a psychic factor referring back to a precursor
of the ego, a zonally unbound center of psychic unity which would
seem to control archetypal constellations, and which seems to be
discernible in the foetal reactions of the twenty-eighth week of pregnancy. It is this zonally unbound psychic factor that becomes the
center of the *unio mentalis*, leading subsequently to the reunion of
unio mentalis to a "glorified body" and the *aurora consurgens* or *unus*

mundus. The tank, serpent-fish and poison reflect the presence of this "latent logos," this Agathodaimon serpent-spirit of unity.

The mystery of this deep phylogenetic substrate in the psyche is experienced not only as the encounter with the animal psyche; in the same place and at the same time it is the meeting with the anima as feminine psychopomp, both as a masculine experience of the unconscious and as a fundamental transformational character of the archetypal feminine. It shows the way to Mercurius and the phoenix — the firebird that first rises from its own ashes in a snake- or worm-like form. This proximity between the anima and the primitive monster, the classic polarity of bird and snake, appears in mythology as a young maid and a monster who are in close proximity to each other and who seem to have a secret understanding. In feminine psychology this "proximity" is felt as a tacit understanding in which feminine conscience may accomplish its purposes.

It is this secret understanding that is overshadowed by "black sulphur" in the "modern woman." For if she is unaware of her anima character, she finds herself in the situation of trying to be a hero-animus, and so, having blocked eros and the approaches to her feeling, she is overshadowed by the monster, by the archaic feminine. This appeared in *A*'s murder of the youth in the Palestine dream. But it is the hero-animus who must lead her forth from a mythological destiny into life and awaken her awareness of her anima nature. Only so can she become a leader of man's soul. This occurs in the "eschatological" passages of the Palestine dream, where her identification with "Pallas" leads her to the reactivation of an archetypal feminine conscience, and so, to a reawakening of her congealed and obtenebrated femininity. For the first transformation must be the awareness of herself in her anima character and her liberation from the monster whose vitality

90

she no longer discerns with her feminine conscience. The second transformation, which follows on her encounter with the hero whom, in a
way, she brings to birth, consists in the *solificatio* which enhances and
fulfills her lunar feminine consciousness. Thus she both generates and
is fertilized by a masculine agency in her soul which aims at insight and
self-awareness. The Negro and the blond youth symbolize this process.
Alchemically speaking, we are looking into the "dark body" of the
Shulamite's ego.

The experience of the fourth function in alchemy is described as
ascent and descent through the seven planetary houses; ascent and
descent, above and below, up and down represent an emotional realization of the opposites. It corresponds to the alchemical image of a
flight between a winged and wingless dragon; in dreams this state appears as climbing a stairway, or as airplanes, or air-journeys, or, as we
have suggested, intercontinental voyages to the other side of the ter-
restial globe and return. The "descent" signifies analysis, the "ascent,"
synthesis. This motif, like the mandala, appears at moments of crisis
and aims at establishing an equilibrium. In our dreams, as we have
noted, the tendency is primarily "descensional" or analytical, in the
sense that it points to an inorganic or mineral level of the *anima mundi*.
Emotionally, the state pictured is regressive and depressional, corresponding to the state of *nigredo* and "dissolution" of the alchemists.
This journey is equivalent to the "voyage of the hero," the crucial
"meeting at the ford," etc. It represents a situation of *transitus*, and
in our dream it appears at the moment of changing from plane to ship,
in proximity to the ominous crab-shaped rock where the unknown
hero dives into the sea. The light of life is extinguished, but he continues his journey in the form of a crab or fish or serpent. Later he will
reappear as a strong wind, as *pneuma*, or as an airman — sometimes
positive, sometimes negative. The elusive Mercurius is both the subject

and object of this *transitus*, both feminine and masculine, both the solvent and the dissolved, both sacrificer and victim, as well as the medium.

The process begins in *nigredo*: melancholy, depression, suffering in the fear, loneliness and wretchedness of human life. Its aim is to unite the powers of above and below, to bring down spiritual powers to the relentless facts of real life, and to produce the poison-panacea, the *medicina catholica*, which also appears in human form as a divine child, as a spagyric foetus, as a youth, or as a hermaphrodite.

Thus consciousness is confronted both with a deepening and an expanding horizon. *"Solutio"* means a loosening of a cramped attitude. A separation of the elements through the agency of the *aqua permanens* occurs, a substance which is always present in the body and is lured out by the "art." This "art" is analysis, and involves an anamnesis and thorough examination of the contents which are the expression or cause of the problematic situation. The solvent agent, the "water," is a soul or spirit, a psychic substance which is applied to the initial material, as we have seen in relation to the pork.

This psychic substance also appears in the asthma, as both the cause and cure of the complaint; and the behavior of the symptom, its alternations and centering, corresponds to the same phenomena as illustrated in the dream-images in which the psychic situation and process are symbolized. For the "centering" of the symptom into the analytical hour is a physiological equivalent to the circular formation of a mandala, and the gradual "extraction" of its symbolic meaning is coordinated to a circulation of psychic energy in the self as it moves out of a level of physiological phenomena and into the level of the psyche as such. Alchemically, it is correlated to white sulphur in feminine psychology; psychologically it is a "psychogonia," a process of soul-creation."

This process constitutes an emergent illumination of consciousness
as by the moon on a dark night. This illumination comes to a certain
extent from the diffuse luminosity, like the phosphorescence of the
moon-lit sea, of the unconscious itself. It leads to the *albedo*. The
moonlight heralds the morning sun — the growing redness or *rubedo*
denoting an increase in the warmth and light and participation of consciousness as it begins to react emotionally to unconscious contents.
At first this state appears as open conflict, fiery and violent, but it
leads eventually to the melting and synthesis of the opposites — the
"marriage" of Sol and Luna. This means that the warring opposites
tend to destroy each other, and in so doing, to give birth to a third
being. The conflict is gradually split-off and becomes its own battle-
field. In *A*'s psychology this appears in the gradual withdrawal of the
conflict-motif of war as we have seen it in the Palestine dream. It
continues in the psychic background in gradually diminishing intensity.

The ascent and descent means the shedding of the compulsive character — the "horoscope" — imprinted on each person at his birth. By
a sort of regressive liberation, one gains maximum consciousness and
so maximum freedom of will. Hence, the compulsions and possession
by the "archons," the archaic unconscious determinants of character,
are loosened. Psychologically, this can appear as a liberation from the
demoralization which sets in when the psychic factors producing neurotic symptoms are taken as unalterable hereditary genetic facts which
it is useless to resist.

There is a final aspect of these two Australia dreams which illustrates
the profundity of their symbolism. This consists in the "contrary motions" in the dreams. In the first journey *A* goes West, following the
course of the sun, and so arrives at the poison panacea. This is the

direction of consciousness, and more precisely, the solar, diurnal consciousness of her contrasexual side. Her journey takes her by way of America, "water," the unconscious, in which Sol is dissolved each night. In the second dream, however, she goes East, counter-clockwise, against the sun. She goes toward Asia, "air," but at a crucial point of passage she must continue her journey by water, facing the ancient dangers confronting one who explores the unknown for the first time.

These contrary motions suggest a fundamental contrast in orientation and dynamism between that of the ego and the self. In her westward journey *A*'s solar consciousness seems at once to enhance itself and yet also to hasten to its own destruction. In the eastward journey, although she moves contrary to the sun and into the origins of her diurnal consciousness, she encounters a profound content of her own feminine nature: the crab-shaped rock in the sea which, although dangerous, is no longer poisonous. It has taken on the primitive form of the *lapis*, and so is an image of the self.

These contrary motions accordingly lead one to suspect that the circulatory motions in the ego and in the self are mirror opposites of each other. Thus if the ego goes eastward, contrary to the course of its solar diurnal consciousness and so, in a sense, *toward* the unconscious, nonetheless the movements of the autonomous contents of the psyche, like the rock, for example, or the asthma, are "emergent," moving *into* a consciousness which is less "of the ego" than witnessed by the ego as one among other luminaries in the inner heaven of the psyche. Hence, the circulation of the self in this case is "clockwise," while that of the ego is "counter-clockwise."

Perhaps this phenomenon led Jung to see the motion of the self in its entirety as clockwise in the "formula diagram" in *Aion*, while the motion of the "nodes" in the formula he saw as counter-clockwise, which is to say, as facing *toward* the motion of the self with its healing influences.

We can follow the mutations of the motifs brought to light in these dreams in others which followed immediately on the last Australia dream.

Two nights later *A* is in the restored family house at Santa Croce. The garden, which forms the atrium of the house, is beautifully green, made of cloth. In the garden there are many cut flowers in small crystal *lacrimariae*. These tiny antique vases have holes in the bottom, but the water does not drain away and the flowers remain ever-living.

The "cloth garden" — the color of which resembles the green blaze of the analyst's desk — means an *opus contra naturam* and a "living woven destiny" associated with the analytical situation. The greenness suggests the "occult" green sulphur which becomes the *prima materia* of the *lapis*. It means an intensification of the creative and procreative energies of spirit and life, or functionally, an intensification of the introverted pole of the sensation function.

In the alchemical tradition, this greenness is "blessed"; as Johannes Steeb says,[5] it is generated in the vegetable kingdom as a result of a fertilizing effect of the spirit of God in the supercelestial waters, giving rise to a fostering, penetrating, nourishing warmth which, combining with light, initiates transforming activities proper to the "soul of the world." This greenness thus corresponds to chlorophyll; it is correlated to light as a transformative activity in vegetable life and is an aspect of that "photosensitivity" to which we have referred. It represents a modification of the healing tomato in the bipontic dream, and we can conjecture that something of the inner warmth and light of the Negro youth has been extracted in this dream.

The anti-natural nature of this greenness also appears in the flower motif. The flowers, cut off from their natural earth roots and from their seasonal ephemerality, go on living "eternally" in the miraculous waters of the spirit – in the *aqua permanens* in the tear-vases, which alludes to the supercelestial waters "springing into eternal life." They also allude to the self and the *lapis*. The possibility for this comes from the wisdom which has been distilled from the *aqua pontica*: the wisdom is derived from the bitterness of the salt tears preserved in the crystal *lacrimariae*. The holes in the bottoms of the crystal vases at once emphasize the miraculous nature of these waters and also permit a "pneumatic communication" between the miraculous waters contained in the vases and the preternatural green of the garden. The holes, in effect, symbolize transcendence and intercommunication.

The sequence illustrated in these three dreams begins and ends in Santa Croce, in the milieu of A's ancestral psyche. Its "restoration" means, as we have seen, that its deep religious significance has become acute. The "journey out" leads to the "poison." But in the last dream the meaning of the poison is revealed. It has acted like a visitation of spirit, bringing to A's inner conflict the healing vitality and wisdom of the self.

The problem of eros with its spirit now becomes the psyche's central interest. In the next dream, a fragment, a young woman named Regine is invoking something or asking for something.

This extremely terse dream nonetheless seemed especially important because of the rather unusual name Regine – which in alchemy is the title of Luna. After considerable searching, it finally emerged that she was the servant in Ibsen's *Ghosts*. The patient's mother had frequently played the role of Mrs. Alving in the play.

The play, as will be remembered, is concerned with the infection

of the son Oswald by syphilis inherited from the father. It ends with
the son's madness, his asking for the sun, while the mother searches
for the poison which he has implored her to administer in the event of
his insanity. Surrounding this tragedy of the Alvings are the moral
problems and hypocracies which, as malignant spirits, settle cloudlike
over the household. Central to these issues is the figure of Pastor
Manders, at once the unconscious illustration, cause and victim of the
critical situation. As a sinister undercurrent there runs the motif of
brother-sister incest in the love of Oswald for Regine, since Regine
is the illegitimate daughter of Oswald's father.

This dream, so laconic, nonetheless sheds a livid light on A's inner
world — on the corruption of the rotting pork, on the specters that
have overshadowed eros, on the meaning of Shakespeare's Sonnets
in her mother's life. And it also points forward, as we shall see. The
motif of the sea assumes a most important part in A's subsequent
dreams. Likewise the figure of a spiritual father emerges — perhaps
a development from Pastor Manders. Finally, the problem of rescuing
her mother's anima character from the poisonous shadow of the Mother
becomes A's central mission.

In the play, the son's insanity appears in his asking for the sun. He
is asking for a curative and warming masculine agency and for a masculine solar world which will make him whole. The positive "balsam"
qualities of red sulphur with the extracted and transmuted Typhonian
and Venerean shadow of the sun are in question here, as we saw, too,
in A's dream of the red dress, the burning bath and the curative pulp
of the tomato. Hence, a masculine homoerotic motif in the play becomes a paraphrase of the latent brother-sister incest motif. The illness
here works as a taboo.

In the dream, it seems plausible to conjecture that Regine is asking

97

for the moon — for a restored feminine consciousness which will coun-
teract the poisoned eros and "dark sun" infecting the psychic environment passed on by the "specters." She is seeking liberation from the
Sol niger which has obtenebrated her feminine consciousness and
turned it into the dark shadow of the mother and the "guardian spirits"
of the Mother's deathly aspect.

In the play this "dark spirit" appears at once as the poisoned eros
passed on by the father and in the morphine with which Mrs. Alving
kills her son. In *A*'s psychology this spirit corresponds to the poison
which she has brought back from Australia and to the life-spirit moving
in the preternatural green of the "cloth garden" at Santa Croce. In the
present dream it heralds the moonrise of *A*'s feminine consciousness
with its mitigating light and phosphorescent luminosity.

In the dream, Regine's asking for the moon sets up a feminine
homoerotic parallel to the masculine homoerotic factor in the play's
termination. Both are paraphrasing resonances striking out from the
incest motif which we have noted, and in each case a spiritualizing
agency is at work. For in both instances the "parallel homoeroticism"
means a curative initiation into a masculine or feminine world and not
sexual behavior. Hence, the dream pictures a splitting process leading
to the differentiation of a consciousness appropriate to a given sex.
Regine asks for the full moon; she invokes the full eros appropriate
to the lunar consciousness specific to her femininity. She asks for it
"from the left," from the side of illegitimacy, unconsciousness, homoeroticism and incest. As in the second Australia dream, Regine faces
into the origins of the diurnal masculine solar consciousness and finds
her answer in the emergent *albedo* qualities of the feminine aspect of
the self.

As a dream symbol Regine is thus *A*'s answer to the problem constellated by the play, in that she asks for a lunar consciousness that will at once "kill" and "heal" the virulent eros of the solar world in her primordial feminine moisture. Here too a *coniunctio* has occurred; and here too a taboo has worked a spiritualizing influence in turning A's attention inward toward her reflective feminine consciousness.

In the play frequent mention is made of "vitality": the vitality of the father leading to the sin with which he filled the monotony of his life, Regine's vitality, and the more sinister aspects of this vitality in the disease, in the mother and the morphine with which she kills her sun-struck son, and in the holocaust of the orphanage, started inadvertently by Pastor Manders. This vitality finds its counterpart in the various manifestations of the arcane substance in A's psychology; its activity, as we have seen, is equally "accidental," ambivalent, and works equally profoundly as a feminine conscience, to bring to birth a spiritually more valid world.

CHAPTER IV

UNIO NATURALIS:
DARK WATER AND FLOWING LIGHT

The problem of eros and spirit reaches a solution in the following dream, which is the last dream in this group. Here, as we observed earlier, we encounter the primary contrasexual factor in the very foundation of *A*'s femininity, the immanent "photosensitivity" and "phosphorescence" which is the aim of her homoeroticism and her lunar consciousness as it appeared in Regine's invocation to the moon. It is also the motive force in the feminine conscience which guides the vicissitudes of eros in her life.

A is in a sort of fast galley like an ancient Greek or Roman ship. They approach the wreck of a large steamship grounded on a submerged rock. It is intact, except that it has no rivets and is about to disintegrate. *A* and her companions board the empty ship, and she hears a small dog crying in one of the cabins. The dog is black, like the one in the photograph of her mother. She rescues it, and they row quickly away, in order not to be sucked under by the breaking up and sinking of the ship. The ship resembled the "Leviathan" in which her parents took their wedding trip.

This dream is of the greatest interest. The ship, which was black and very large, has come to grief on the crab-shaped rock of which the Captain warned in the dream of the voyage to Australia: that is, the negative mother hidden in the unconscious. The ship is unriveted:

100

it is held together "from within" by an inner center of unity. Once this center has been "extracted" — the little black dog in the photograph of *A*'s mother — the ship can break up and sink. It returns to the archetypal feminine, a sacrifice to the Terrible Mother who has overshadowed *A*'s experience of her femininity.

The swiftly rowed galley signifies a return to a more ancient and mythological relation to the unconscious. *A* is embarked on a "heroic voyage" like Odysseus, or more precisely, on a "sacred embassy" in which she rescues the soul of her mother — the little black dog — from its possession by the shadow of the archaic dragon-like feminine. The danger here is that *A* might identify with the black ship and the dark animus of the Terrible Mother instead of saving the dog, and so fall victim to the crab and the demonic animus in the shadow of the Terrible Mother. Psychologically, the danger would consist in a violent burst of rage followed by a disastrous depression with suicidal impulses. In these conditions, the rage would reflect the rabid, hydrophobic potentialities of the dog, so that the "soul of the shadow" would not only remain unredeemed but would regress to a morbid state of infection which would kill the divine child in herself. Here *A* is "confronting the dragon." Her role is somewhat like that of a masculine hero in this regard: she is freeing her anima character from the ancestral neurosis of possession, and this is what, among other things, the dog symbolizes.

The dog is the central symbol in this dream. It elucidates the nature of what we might call an "ancestral neurosis," a sort of ethnic shadow infecting *A*'s feminine eros. The dream deepens the meaning of the homosexual undertones of "Regine's invocation to the moon." For the dog is "the voice of the moon"; and it gives us the key to *A*'s characteristic lesbian fantasies in which she identifies

101

with a man – usually elderly – pursuing and violating one or more young girls – frequently Negresses.

This appears in an image from Gnosticism: a woman in the likeness of a dog is pursued by an ithyphallic grey-haired man. She is described as "Persephone's *phlúa*" and is named "Dark Water." The ithyphallic old man is called "Flowing Light." He is a synonym for Hermes Kyllenios.

We have thus arrived at a fundamental point of reduction in the animus factor – the solar component – in *A*'s psychology: a factor which we have seen in the balsam qualities of the tomato, in the "green cloth garden," as well as in a personified form in the hydraulic engineer, the Negro youth and the blond youth in the two Australia dreams, and finally, in Oswald as a background presence in the Regine dream.

The black girls which *A* pursues are the dark "Ethiopian" anima-aspect of Adam. They are the "dark waters" of the first day of Creation, or the "black Shulamite" of alchemistic symbolism. They refer back to a pre-Eve world, where the Earth – Havvah or Eve – was covered by the dark waters over which the spirit moved as an incubating warmth. *A*, on the other hand, identifies with her contrasexual aspect, the transformative mercurial principle which appears ambiguously, at once as "light" and yet also as the activated darkness of matter, like the dark and light heroes in the Australia dreams. *A*'s primary femininity is still in a state of unconsciousness and projection; it becomes perceptible only indirectly, through her identification with the "flowing light" of her contrasexual mentality – the ithyphallic Old Man who is born, fish-like, from precisely those "dark waters."

For "Flowing Light" is lunar rather than solar. He is the lucent reflection of a lunar, feminine consciousness in the "dark waters" of

her primordial nature. He is the "flowing phosphorescence" to which
we have referred, the immanent luminosity of spirit in the dark waters
of femininity which turns foam into silver and clothes fish in cold
flame in the dark waters of the sea on an August night. He symbolizes,
in fact, the native luminosity of the unconscious, Mercurius in his aqueous aspect; he is a heatless "luminosity as such," an immemorial inner
"photosensitivity" borne in the plasm of *bios*, through which feminine
vitality projects itself in the millenary reflections of the psyche's most
ancient processes of experience. "Flowing Light," as a native luminousness
and "photosensitivity" in the biological psyche, links back to a mutation in the phylogenetic origins of animal life as profound in its consequences as the development of chlorophyll in plants. Perhaps the
common origin of cerebral and epidermal cells in the blastular stage
of the embryo reflects this fundamental development in the grey dawn
of life.

The dog into which the archetypal feminine has turned herself is
the dark side of the moon. It is always linked in some way to the
childless Persephone and her chosen friend, Hecate, the negative sor-
ceress goddess of miscarriage, child sacrifice, infanticide, suicide. Her
symbols are the torch, whip and dog. Selene, as "dog" and "bitch,"
speaks with the voice of a dog. The scavenger, necrophagous function
of dogs links them to death and the underworld, so that they are closely
linked as symbols to Persephone, the dark moon-goddess of death.

The Furies, too, appear as serpents and dogs. They punish sins of
violence against the Mother. Hecate as deadly Mother, goddess of
nightmares, night, phantoms, madness and "moon sickness," appears
in the form of a man-eating lamia, as vampire, as serpent, or as a dog.
She receives sacrifices at cross-roads or three-forked intersections where
suicides are buried. Like the Erinyes she forms part of the triple-goddess,

and guards the treasure which is life; hence, she is also identified with Rhea, here presented as the underworld all-Mother in her negative, destructive, deathly aspect. Yet, as the goddess of death, she also points toward life: the immaterial life of spirit.

Hence the dog — associated with epilepsy, madness and illnesses of the spleen — nonetheless also has a curative aspect and is a regular companion of Aesculapius, the God of healing who, while mortal, raised a man from the grave and at Hades' behest was struck down by Jove's thunderbolt. The dog's curative aspect as the "inner unity" of the ship in our dream shows that it is a development of the Agathodaimon serpent, the curative germ of unity in the *prima materia* — the "dark waters" — of Luna's chthonic femininity, her earth-shadow.

In *Mysterium Coniunctionis* Jung has given an extended account of the symbolic meaning of the dog in the alchemistic paradigm. It symbolizes the animal side of King Sol and Luna, that is to say, psychic processes transpiring in the instinctual sphere: exclusively animal reactions and bestial uncontrolled affects. As the theriomorphic shadow of Sol it represents the shadow side of a masculine consciousness and has such synonyms as "lion," "unclean body," "red sulphur," and *"ignis gehennalis."* As the theriomorphic aspect of Luna the dog appears along with such synonyms as "moon bitch," "cold serpent," "basilisk," "dark water," and "black salt." Thus the dog is the fruit of a *matrimonium luminarium* at a regressive animal level. The royal pair can only appear after their animal passions — the dragon, the snake, the rabid dog, etc. — have either been killed or killed each other. For, as Jung says, there is evil and darkness in the parents which can only come to light in their offspring. And so collectivity, childish, brutally short-sighted goals of pride and concupiscence which have hardened into a *habitus* reveal themselves as a sort of hydrophobic dog. And this is one aspect of the

104

little black dog in our dream. It has come into being along with Regine's invocation to the moon and Persephone's "midnight ululations." It condenses into itself solar and lunar agencies at a bestial level in which evil has hardened into a *habitus* and the diseased eros passed on by the parents acts like the foaming rage of a rabid dog, or the venereal component in the Typhonian *ignis gehennalis*.

The dog accordingly represents a central symbol of possession in *A*'s psychology. It condenses into itself not only the masculine and feminine agencies of an archetypal consciousness, but also the dark, nonmanifest, shadow-side of those agencies. It personifies black sulphur and black salt as a sort of bilateral possession, as a raging animal drive which thwarts conscious will and feeling, and which accentuates the tension that exists not only between the shadow and the self but also between masculine and feminine agencies moving in the self. Hence, the dog personifies a compounded shadow, an *umbra solis* both in Sol and Luna which eclipses the true light in both of them. The dog thus personifies a novilunary situation and a dual eclipse. It becomes the *Sol niger*, the "shadow of the sun" which is the "heat of the moon," compact of furious animosity and cold rage.

Behind the images of our dream, therefore, a conjunction of Sol and Luna in their unfavorable aspects seems to have taken place. The "flowing light" of a pre-solar consciousness has its dangerous aspects of pride and concupiscence and lunatic berserker rage. Yet the "dark waters" sacred to Diana in her new moon state can also be very deceptive in that Luna may be unaware of the darkness in herself. Then Diana's huntress aspect takes over and destroys the eros in herself.

At this juncture, there bursts forth the always latent hydrophobia of the dog. The dog becomes rabid, afflicted with madness and the

105

darkness of the new moon — the *Novilunium*. The mad dog symbolizes psychic disturbance; a fear of the unconscious infects the infant self, the divine child, in the personality.

The rabid dog is evil itself, yet it is assuaged by Diana's spiritual side — symbolized by winged creatures and pneumatic symbols; through this influence the dog is transformed and becomes an eagle at the *Plenilunium*. Spiritual love — the doves of Diana, Astarte, Venus, Ishtar — makes its appearance and points to a *connubium* of spirit with the waters dedicated to the Virgin and Diana. A winged, aerial *pneuma* moving in the supercelestial waters of spirit penetrates the earth, as in our dream image of the *lacrimariae*. A healing miracle takes place, like the angel which descends and moves the waters of the pool of Bethesda.

The dog, as we have said, is the fruit of a union of Sol and Luna. And these luminaries symbolize certain fundamental psychological facts. On the one hand is Sol as opposed to Luna, or two types of consciousness in opposition to the shadow and the contrasexual component in the personality. But on the other hand, both Sol and Luna are projections, for both have their origin in the "dark body" of the ego from which consciousness itself is projected. This projection is the equivalent of a cosmogony, the "creation of a world," for the advent of consciousness is symbolized as the coming of light in creation myths. Hence, the little black dog symbolizes the shadow side of the ego, the archaic darkness which must be "extracted" and elucidated in the birth of a new mental world. For consciousness has its origin in the shadow of the self, of which the ego is a personification, and is projected as a luminous sheen on the dark waters of the unconscious natural world.

Hence, two cosmogonies are set in opposition: on the one hand the "natural cosmogony," the *unio naturalis* of the unconscious natural world, and on the other the "second" or "psychic" cosmogony, the creation of the world as a differentiated experience by the dawning of the ego's consciousness. Luna is the link between these two cosmogonies. Through her "feminine solar" and "masculine lunar" aspects she reaches back to the grey origins of life, to a solvent photosensitive agency which links the natural world as experienced by the unconscious to the mental world as perceived by consciousness in both its "sulphur" and "salt" aspects.

The dog accordingly concentrates into itself symbolic meanings which belong to a physiological mythology and which allude to agencies in the body's life. But it also has a cosmological referent and concentrates into itself two "worlds," two consciousnesses. This appears in its astrological aspect, where it figures as Sirius, the Dog Star. By nature, the dog is closest to the primal waters of the unconscious from which it rises. It then assumes a solar nature, for Helios, the sun, appears in the second house in the form of a dog, as the "begetter." In the twelfth house Helios returns to the sea as a crocodile, as a dragon-like aquatic monster finishing in the crab-shaped rock in our dream.

At the peak of the sun's journey come the *canicula*, when the rabid canine aspect of Sol bursts forth. At this point the canine aspect of Sol becomes the predatory instrument of Artemis. The black sun, the sultry heat of Luna, irrupts, obscuring the true solar consciousness, bringing with it ancient memories of the waxing and waning of a "masculine" moon in a "feminine" solar world, a "moon" which, as "son," was the symbol of menstrual cycles, pregnancy, and was also related to the glowing nocturnal light of the cat's eye by which the dark, predatory, feline instincts of a nocturnal animal world were perceived.

At this point the dog must be destroyed. Archaic bestial passions moving in its blood, both solar and lunar, producing a rabid hydrophobic consciousness at war with itself, must be transformed. The alchemical picture gives us a parable for the union of opposites. Out of chaos, madness, darkness and ravenous evil instincts, a new light must be born, but this is possible only through the death of the animal demon in humankind. Through this death and atonement, Mercurius is constellated as a fountain of renewal, as a sort of zonally unbound, protective awareness in the total psyche, working as a continual flow of interest to and from the unconscious.

This center exists, as we have seen, in *A*'s asthma; in the menstrual disturbance the lunar aspect of the dog as a sort of cat-like "son" was also present as a mercurial factor. Here, in our dream, this center appears again in the image of the little dog which holds together the unriveted leviathan.

In alchemical language, one must now open the belly of the moon bitch and "extract the darkness" which is nonetheless the *succus vitae*. This means that one must extract the spirit or soul, and so bring to consciousness contents hidden in the unconscious — a spirit symbolized also by sulphur, salt, menstrual blood, or *aqua permanens*.

This *"succus"* is frequently not an authentic unconscious content, but rather shows the effect of such a content on the conscious mind, capturing its attention and working toward integration. It constitutes a sort of "vital attention" which in ego-consciousness appears in the adhesion of the mind to its object, as conscious will and memory, and as love, but which has roots extending down through compulsive layers of the personality where it appears as the motive force of a sort of animal faith, and still deeper, in the tropisms and arcs of neural processes and as the germinal component in cellular life. We have seen its activity not only in *A*'s compulsions, but also in her physiological and sexual disturbances, as well as in her dreams and fantasies. This vital attention is thus a sort of unifying, inborn, protective awareness moving in symptom-formation, in fantasy- and dream-life, and in the psychoid processes of the physiological psyche. It is the archaic progenitor, the *materia*, and the aim of processes moving out of the body's life into the life of the psyche as such, and it reaches its climax in the will, the reason, the feeling and the perceptions of an individuated personality. *Succus vitae* symbolizes the subjective factor — the vital attention of consciousness as an archetypal aspect of the psyche — which acts like an incubating warmth, warming and activating the unconscious and breaking down the barriers between the ego's consciousness and the unconscious.

The opening of the belly of the moon-bitch means opening the matrix which contains an essential part of the personality. Sol and Luna in this regressive, rabid aspect must be transformed in an *opus ad album* which belongs to the moon-nature and in an *opus ad rubedum* which belongs to the solar nature. In the human world this appears as the Adept and the *Soròr Mystica*. The arcane substance is the symbol and instrument of this process. If consciousness accepts it, the arcane substance appears as positive, if not, as negative. If the arcane substance is split into two natures, it is seen as two incompatible tendencies and is taken to be two different things — as rotting pork on the one hand, and as a clever little black dog on the other.

From this it is clear that Mercurius is a projection. He symbolizes the unconscious itself as the subjective factor, the source and maker of images which is totally present without ever being totally exhausted in any image. Mercurius is an absolutely primitive concept, alluding to the unconscious itself where nothing is differentiated, and yet he works as a "living spirit" and active principle which must appear in consciousness in differentiated form. Hence, *Mercurius duplex*, as active, appears as Sol, as passive, as Luna. Consciousness requires a dark, latent, nonmanifest side — the unconscious from which consciousness, the diurnal aspect of the cosmic Nous, is born like the day star, and to which it returns each night. This duality of psychic life is the prototype and archetype for the Sol-Luna symbolism.

Now, in the light of the above remarks, let us return to our dream.

To begin with, the ship becomes a sort of "vessel of the unconscious," a matrix, a leviathan which has foundered on the submarine crab-rock which is here revealed as a maleficent aspect of Luna. Yet in its belly it carries a unifying center which is essential to personality. Once this center is taken out or "extracted," the leviathan goes into solution and sinks back into unconscious depths. A *coniunctio* has taken place. Here the solar and dark aspects of the hero as we saw them in the Australia dreams — the Negro and the blond youth — are joined in the "hot belly of the monster"; but in our dream they are rescued less by their own efforts, as is the case in the typical solar myth, than by a heroic aspect of *A* herself as feminine psychopomp.

At this level, the swiftly rowed galley carrying *A* represents the vital flow of interest, the *succus vitae*, attracted by an authentic content of the unconscious contained in the belly of the stranded leviathan.

But at this juncture, the extraction of the dog from the ship means that the dog itself becomes the *succus vitae*. A transformation has occured, so that the dog itself becomes the carrier of vital interest and consciousness and leads to an ulterior penetration of the arcane substance into the dark world of the feminine. Femininity itself and a primordial feminine consciousness become the center of interest and the *succus vitae*. In other words, the interior life of the dog itself attracts interest, and in this attraction the dog itself becomes the volatile substance of consciousness, pointing toward the "flowing light" which it attracts.

At this point, therefore, we enter into the inner life of *A*'s homo-sexual fantasies and the vicissitudes of the moon-psychology to which they belong. They constitute the *succus vitae* of the dog and point toward the Persephone-Hermes Kyllenois image from Gnosticism.

Here the feminine aspect of the arcane substance, the lunar, passive aspect of Mercurius, takes the form of a dog. "Dark Water" — Perseph-one, dog-like with her snakey, deathly, streaming hair — now becomes "the voice of the moon" and the "heat of the sun" and makes her ap-pearance as the moon-bitch. And she is pursued by the masculine ag-gressive aspect of Mercurius as Hermes Kyllenios, the ithyphallic old man named "Flowing Light." Here again the *succus vitae* or Mercurius has split up into dual form. Again, it is less a case of different entities than diverse manifestations of the same thing. The tension between opposites in the subjective factor, rendered acute because of the polar-ity which has emerged between different levels of itself, has now en-tered and indeed caused awareness. A specifically feminine sort of consciousness becomes perceptible, first as an object of interest, sub-sequently as a deeply buried subject of interest, spirating in the ances-tral deposits of the phylogenetic psyche.

A's identification with "Flowing Light" means that she has iden-tified with an archaic complex of a masculine order, a principle of lunar masculine consciousness which is contained in her contrasexual side, and which projects its "flowing light," its liquid luminosity, its innate photosensitivity, onto her split-off feminine substance. An archaic darkness has descended on the waters of her feminine nature, producing that "hydrophobia" which is the fateful illness latent in the dog. This is the source of her animus possession, her compulsive rages and her aggressive impulsiveness. She is carried into the shadow-world

111

of Hecate — the goddess of abortions, infanticide, suicide, phantoms, delusions, rages and depressions.

Thus, all of those elements which we have mentioned — the red dress, the *aqua pontica*, the murdered youth, the corrupted pork; the salt, the red-sulphur, and the "lion" syndromes; the serpent-poison, the livid purple, as well as the tears of the *lacrimariae* and the infected eros of Reg̈ne and the sun — have been constellated. All of these have coalesced in this dream. They become the Furies, twin sisters of Aphrodite, born of the blood of the severed phallus of Uranus. They are the punishers of violent sins against the Mother, the feminine self, and they become the motive force of the compulsion of *A*'s possession by the animus. Adam as the "Ethiopian," in his black aspect, the saturnine maleficent aspect of the *Vetula* — the Old Witch — has been constellated, and in the Negress in *A*'s fantasies the shadow of *Vetula* herself has come to life. The ancient seething passions of pride and concupiscence in the shadow of the feminine have been activated as the feminine background — the "dark water" — of the masculine aspect of *A*'s psyche.

Yet at this point we must notice a significant aspect of our dream which points in another direction. There seems to be a "secret understanding" between *A* and the stranded monster — the leviathan and the rock; a tacit agreement that the ship shall not go to pieces until the dog has been rescued, or the eros in "Dark Water" has been enlightened. A sort of feminine conscience moves through the whole. This acts like a *succus vitae* of another sort, a "feminine consciousness" contemplating the immemorial passions of itself — or the self-experience of the feminine as illuminated reflectively by its contrasexual aspect.

From the point of view of "Dark Water" with the canine nature in its positive aspect, it is rather "Flowing Light" who becomes an extraneous and genuinely unconscious content that awakens her to reflection and attracts to herself that luminous factor which she herself both projects and elicits. Her anima-character comes to the fore and re-vitalizes the flowing light of the feminine's ancient "masculine" experience of the unconscious. Here, the positive side of the Negro has its origin — as the *warmth* of luminosity, which is the opposite contained in the heatless phosphorescence of "Flowing Light," an opposite dramatized in the ardor of his ithyphallic aspect.

From this point of view, "Dark Water" becomes the creative force of feminine consciousness which transforms the light of the sun into the cool warmth of her reflective lunar nature. The dog accordingly symbolizes not only an encounter with the animal soul but also the encounter with the anima character as psychopomp, as a transformative agency in the psychology of both sexes.

Perhaps for this reason there are no rabid symptoms in the little dog. Its hydrophobic aspects have been burned away in the bipontic waters of the Red Sea. Here, the situation is one in which the feminine soul of the mother is being rescued from the shadow of the archaic feminine. And if this is a heroic task, this heroism is specifically feminine and consists precisely in the secret understanding of a feminine conscience which moves her to redeem the mother's soul from the shadow, rather than to slay the dragon which contains and nourishes it. A redemptive, curative influence is at work in the depths of A's feminine psyche.

The galley in this dream has a special character. It has something of the numinosity attached to the "Paralus" and "Salaminia," the sacred Athenian racing galleys used on sacred embassies, the crews of which were free men notable for their antagonism to oligarchy. Something of A's own rebelliousness in the face of conventional

113

opinion perhaps finds expression here and differentiates her voyage from the exploratory voyages of Ulysses. The galley therefore symbolizes the motive energy and purposive flow of an Athena-like divine wisdom in *A*'s personality, linking together Olympian and pre-Olympian aspects of her feminine consciousness.

This view is supported by the emotional tonality of the dream. For, as *A* said, the flashing oars and white foam of the galley seemed like wings, and a stiff wind blew in their faces as they flew away from the now gutted and disintegrating ship. The same feeling came from the very first dream of her analysis, where some sailing vessels of fishermen seemed like angels with white wings as they rescued her and her brother from a sinking boat.

This must mean that the wings of the dove, the pneumatic spirit of Diana, the Aesculapian aspect of dog and serpent, are also present, heralding the *plenilunium* of a full lunar consciousness. The mythological battle between a winged and wingless dragon which has gone on in the green and watery depths of the unconscious has been resolved in favor of the galley, a "winged dragon" which bears the heroic daughter-anima, but which does not dissociate itself from the bosom of the sea that bears it and with which it holds an enduring tryst. In the galley's swift motion, in its flashing wing-like bow waves, the sea and the wind hold tryst together, and in its sinuous wake, and in the foam of the sea's breaking waves, the wind's feet shine along the sea. A union of spirit-wind and sea has occurred, and this is the very heart and central *coniunctio* of Mercurius himself. In each ruffling of the surface of the sea, in each splashing surge, sky and sea unite, and love is reborn and regenerated from the serene and mindless face of a pre-Uranian Aphrodite. This would seem to be the inner meaning of "Dark Water" and "Flowing Light" and of the deeper reaches stirred to motion in our dream; it points to a transformation of Cyprian Venus and the Typhonian Sea.

We can thus trace the mutations of the *succus vitae* through several levels of extraction: from rock to ship; from ship to dog; and from dog to "Dark Waters" illuminated by the "Flowing Light" which she elicits and attracts to herself.

This means that in feminine psychology the *unio mentalis*, the extraction of the psyche from the corporeality of the body, takes place in a special way. It is not a case of violent rupture, a killing of a mother- and father-dragon, as is the case in masculine psychology, but rather a sort of pre-concerted theft which is rather a transformation and emergent growth, based on the secret agreement of a feminine conscience that is indifferent to individuals but profoundly aware of the inner vitality of *bios*. It is this ancient wisdom which *A* has won from the "Old Woman," the *Vetula*, the crab-shaped rock, and it carries them free of the vortex and suction of the dying leviathan.

A's dream of the galley and the rescue of the dog corresponds mythologically to a sacred embassy that amounts to a visitation of spirit. It permits the rescue of the archaic, transformational anima-aspect of *A*'s mother's soul from the shadow of the Primordial Mother. It is a fundamentally feminine heroic action, however, in that it is less a "theft" than an act of transformation and regeneration requiring exertion within the context of a tacit and extremely unsentimental agreement. A feminine conscience moving in the archetypal feminine itself establishes a numinous "moment," a synchronicity, a tacit suspension of hostilities in order that this ritual creative action may be accomplished.

———————

With the constellation of the figures "Dark Water" and "Flowing

Light," a fundamental level in A's personality has been reached which becomes a turning point or point of reversal in the analytical process. A tendency, proximally oriented toward instinct and the physiological life of *bios*, here reaches its goal; a conjunction of two aspects of a feminine lunar consciousness has occurred. As we shall see, henceforth the energy of the psyche tends to take a distal orientation toward spirit which reaches its most majestic formulation in the last dream of the next chapter, where the sapphire floor of an underground gallery of a sacred island symbolizes the transfiguration of "Dark Water" and "Flowing Light" into the *aqua permanens,* the divine waters "above the heavens," the "sapphire stone" which God placed over the abyss of Creation.

This reversal first appeared in the contrary motion of the second Australia dream, in which the disintegrative effects of the poison panacea became evident. Previous to the appearance of this deep psychic factor, we saw it primarily in its solar, Typhonian and Venerean aspect: first, in the red dress, the dare, the burning water and the curative tomato, and next, in the sulphurous and saline agencies brought to bear on the rotting pork in the Palestine dream. The fundamental tension in the personality, prefigured in the problematic situation elucidated in the "bipontic" Red Sea predicament, reaches its clearest statement in the two Australia dreams. Thenceforth predominantly lunar saline agencies are at work. The green cloth garden, with its *lacrimariae* at Santa Croce, represents the first spiritualization of this conflict of contraries. In the ancestral environment of Santa Croce, with the religious connotations of its name, *Sal* as the motive force in a feminine lunar consciousness produces a "bitterness," which nonetheless gives birth to a comforting wisdom.

Finally, in Regine's invocation to the moon, the whole problem of a feminine eros, a feminine consciousness, and a feminine conscience, is set against the contents of Ibsen's *Ghosts*, so that the collective consciousness of a masculine solar world acts as the backdrop for processes interior to *A*'s femininity and the pre-solar contrasexual component in that femininity.

The dream of the wrecked leviathan and the little black dog represents the termination of this process. In linking up *A*'s lesbian fantasies to the ancient Gnostic image of Persephone in her canine aspect pursued by an ithyphallic Hermes, we have been able to conjecture the deeper meaning of the homosexual motif in *A*'s personality. Its aim is to achieve unity with a content fundamental to her femininity, and the whole drama is interior to that femininity. Finally, through the names attached to the figure of the dog and the old man, we have been able to set the superhuman divine aspect of these figures opposite their subhuman aspects, reaching down into the psychoid processes of the physiological psyche. These names, therefore, have worked as "divine *logoi*," as symbols, in the deepest sense, pointing toward a reality in the depths of the psyche lying beyond our direct experience.

We have regarded the components of this conjunction of "Dark Water" and "Flowing Light" as symbolizing a mutation in the earliest development of life as portentous in its consequences as the development of chlorophyll in plants, and indeed, it may be considered as a parallel to that development, working out in the specifically animal realm.

Here too alchemy seems to have had penetrating intuitive insights. In connection with the dream of the green cloth garden, we referred to the seventeenth-century Johann Steeb and his view of the "blessed greenness" as a transformative activity stemming from light. At this point it is appropriate to cite him in greater detail. He speaks of the fostering warmth of the Holy Spirit in the supercelestial waters, ren-

117

dering them "milky, so to speak" – in our symbolism, having something of the qualities of "white sulphur" and "phosphorus." This virtue, he continues, penetrates and nourishes all things, and, combining with light, generates the mercurial serpent in the mineral kingdom of the lower regions, the blessed greenness (chlorophyll) in the vegetable kingdom, and a formative virtue in the animal kingdom. "Thus, the supercelestial spirit of the waters, united in marriage with light, may justly be called the soul of the world." "The outflowings of light," he adds, "are absorbed in the capacious depths of the darksome lower waters." [1]

Steeb is here pointing to soul as a central reality, the arcane substance of life and its transformations, soul, which is not identical to mind or spirit, nor yet identical to matter.

Within this context, the homosexual element appearing in *A*'s psychology can be considered to have a specific function. Its aim would seem to be to achieve union through *A*'s contrasexual aspect with a feminine subject of consciousness appropriate to her feminine sex. As we have observed, this has involved a regression to a pre-solar world and a "pre-animus" state, during which *A*'s fixations are gradually dissolved, and she is reduced to the *prima materia* of her femininity. This has required not only the differentiation of her contrasexual aspect, but also the "extraction of a shadow" which lies in the very ground-plan of her personality. Yet, even if the aim of this process is to arrive at a motive force of consciousness appropriate to her feminine nature, nonetheless it has also required the penetration to a level of the psyche lying deeper than sexual differences. Most deeply, the finality of this process consists in a *"psychogonia,"* the self-penetration of soul – the psyche – as the central creative reality and the arcane substance of human life.

Contrasexual factors in an archetypal consciousness here tend to merge in a deep subjective factor moving in the physiological uniformity of the body's life, a factor common to both men and women, but anterior to the differentiation of the anima and animus. And it is with the constellation of this unifying vital attention, this deep reflective capacity, this "photosensitivity" and "innate luminosity" in the depths of the soul, that curative influences are activated aiming at the restoration of a psychic balance which in turn will form the basis for a consciousness appropriate to A's femininity. Thus, if in the present dream psychic energies have been touched which lie deeper than sexual differences, nonetheless those same energies appear as the motive force of a consciousness which must be experienced in differentiated form as appropriate to a masculine or feminine nature.

From the standpoint of our alchemical paradigm, not only have the Typhonian and Venerean aspects of a solar red sulphur done their work, but also a regressive aspect of Luna has entered into the scene, so that "Flowing Light" has been dissolved in the "Dark Waters" of her chthonic, sublunary primeval moisture. In this conjunction, therefore, the shadow of the mother is enlightened by an inborn phosphorescence. Transformative processes are initiated in which the mother renews herself in the anima character of an archetypal femininity, at once the animal psyche and the anima as a transformational drive in both sexes.

Alchemistically speaking, therefore, the process shows the appearance of "white sulphur" reactions in the personality. "Flowing Light" is a synonym for this — "white sulphur" with its introverted, "coagulating" effects. It is a symbol for the immanent luminosity and photosensitivity of which we have spoken, giving rise to cooling second thoughts and generating reflective ideas which are, as it were, the "eternal essences" hidden in the images and emotional patterns of the arcane substance in its primitive aspect.

It is for this reason, perhaps, that the names, the *logoi*, of "Dark Water" and "Flowing Light" are so profoundly symbolic. For they exhibit "white sulphur" as the motive force in a moist feminine consciousness, whether in the anima of a masculine mind or in the anima character and contrasexual component of the feminine; this "white sulphur" is fundamentally reflective in character, linking together "red sulphur" and "salt" and aiming at the restoration of the highly valued ideas of consciousness to their context in the archetype.

This has appeared on two levels of transformation. On one level, it has consisted in lifting certain contents out of the level of physiological phenomena and into the level of psychic experience. Here, pain and discomfort acquire psychic identity as "suffering." The second level, as we shall see, consists in giving suffering meaning as the motive energy and *prima materia* of moral experience. This latter development we have already seen prefigured in the *pudor* to which we have alluded. This development accordingly would seem to reflect the activity of a moral archetype which is emergent from a state of latency, from a state of latent consciousness and latent projection; its potential differentiation is already implicit in the Sol-Luna paradigm. This is the wisdom to which salt and sulphur would lead, and it moves as the arcane substance in the feminine conscience which lies at the root of eros.

The asthma has served as the symbolic indicator of this process of "extraction" as it works out in the physiological psyche. Its "centering" has exhibited it as the physiological equivalent for the formation of a mandala, and as a symbol of the arcane substance as a moist, curative, feminine spirit. With the constellation of "Dark Water" and "Flowing Light," the asthma, much attenuated, had concentrated itself definitively into the first minutes of the analytical hour. 'Dark Water" and

120

"Flowing Light," merging in the reflective activities of "white sulphur."
would seem to be the motive force in this process.

The asthma, "Flowing Light" and "Dark Water" represent various
formulations of the *succus vitae*, the subjective factor, the non-zonally
bound vital attention and protective awareness exhibited by the total
psyche in relation to the body as object. The union of this *succus vitae*
with the effect of the body gives rise to a new psychic fact which consists precisely in the withdrawing of disturbing projections from the
body's life and in the establishment of a new and expanded psychic
balance. Functionally, we have seen this process as located in the introverted aspect, the "contradictory pole," of the dominant extraverted sensation function. The opposition of these orientations has
meant that the outwardly directed reality-sense of the ego-centered,
object-oriented, waking consciousness is counter-balanced by an in-
wardly oriented, million-year-old consciousness, an innate luminosity
and photosensitivity which is non-zonal and belongs to the total psyche.

In the asthma, therefore, this archetypal consciousness is exhibited
in its phylogenetic aspect, as an instinctual activity reaching down into
the tropisms and cellular processes of the physiological psyche. In
other words, at this point the archetype is exhibited in its instinctual
aspect and in those activating "situations" in which it "acquires experience." As we shall see at the end of the next chapter, the archetype of consciousness constellated in "Dark Water" and "Flowing
Light," and condensed into the asthma, will be exhibited in its "eternal," spiritual aspect.

It now becomes incumbent on us to offer a tentative explanation
for *A*'s psychological situation as we find it at this point. And here
Jung's reflections on the sympathetic nervous system can perhaps
offer us a solution. [2]

For, as he points out, the sympathetic nervous system is radically different in origin and function from the cerebrospinal system. The latter reaches its climax in the ego complex. It is outwardly oriented toward objects and governs our adaptation to the world of objects. It plays on surfaces, experiencing things as "outside," and exhibits the ego as the "zonal center" of the experience of an "outside field."

The sympathetic system, on the other hand, maintains the balance of life. It experiences things as "insides," and experiences itself as an "inside." As far as the ego and the cerebrospinal system are concerned, the sympathetic nervous system is the milieu of the collective unconscious *par excellence*. It is "non-zonal," embracing the collective unconscious as a deposit of world processes which, as Jung says, are embedded in the structure of the brain and in the sympathetic nervous system itself, and it constitutes a totality which gives a sort of timeless and eternal world picture that counterbalances our conscious, momentary picture of the world. It gives a mirror-image of a world that has an "inside" as well as an "outside" and acts as a timeless present, expressing the deepest and most subjective recesses of the psyche.

As Jung observes in reflecting on the sort of diffuse consciousness which persists even in cases of severe brain injury or states of deep coma, the sympathetic nervous system can evidently form perceptions and thoughts quite as well as the cerebrospinal system, and in these circumstances it offers itself as the possible carrier of the psychic functions. Hence, he was led to the hypothesis that in the normal unconsciousness of sleep, dreams have their deepest origin primarily in the activity of the unsleeping sympathetic system rather than in the activity of the sleeping cortex.

From this point of view, "Flowing Light" and "Deep Water," as exhibiting a non-zonal *succus vitae*, as well as the asthma as rooted in the activity of the introverted pole of the sensation function, would refer to this "million-year-old consciousness" coded into the vitality of *bios*, which finds expression in the experience of the sympathetic nervous system. The activity of the sympathetic system would thus underlie the "reversal," the "contrary motion," of the second Australia dream, in which the motion of the solar, diurnal consciousness of the ego gives us a mirror-image, a "reflection," of the motion of the self.

The experience of the sympathetic system constitutes "the other," as far as the waking ego's consciousness is concerned. It manifests the spatial and temporal relativity of the unconscious, its diffuse luminosity, and its irrational independence of the categories of space, time and causality which govern the thinking of the waking ego conscious. It manifests itself in causally non-connected but meaningful events which appear in synchronicity-phenomena, which appeared in the "dare" in the bipontic dream and in the "accident" in the Palestine dream, where a "latent logos" precipitated a "mythological" situation of conflict into an eschatological destinal inner process.

"Dark Water" and "Flowing Light" would therefore refer to the activities reaching their climax in the sympathetic nervous system as it maintains the balance of life, as the radically "other," and as the carrier of an archetypal consciousness which is projected in the psychologem of Sol and Luna. It would provide the milieu from which the ego can be viewed as from "outer space," in both its light and dark aspects, as both object and subject, as a relatively constant personification of the self. It embodies the phylogenetic aspect of that non-zonal "observing" consciousness which appears in dreams of self-observation, where one is aware of oneself as dreaming. In such dreams, the memory of the consciousness which is evoked, although bearing an analogy to the consciousness of the waking ego, should nonetheless be taken symbolically, that is, as referring to an archetypal consciousness experienced by the ego in its aspect as a personification of the self, and hence, as located in the shadow of the waking ego's experience of its consciousness.

With the constellation of "Dark Water" and "Flowing Light," therefore, this deepest recess of subjective life has been tapped, giving rise to the reflective activities of "white sulphur" in *A*'s personality.

At this point, by way of conclusion to this chapter, I would like to allude briefly to recent researches in bioluminescence, the scientific equivalent to what we have called phosphorescence. I shall not go into the complexities of its distribution in the plant and animal world and the chemical problems involved. It is enough to say that in the plant world it is exhibited by bacteria and fungi, and in animal form, by insects as well as by tiny organisms such as flagellates, radiolarians, hydroids, sponges, crustaceans, clams, snails and certain species of fish — the only vertebrates exhibiting bioluminescence. Its light is like normal light, except that it has no infra-red or ultra-violet or penetrating rays and that less than one per cent of the energy released in the chemical reaction takes the form of heat. It is thus a cold light and extremely efficient in light production. It can affect photographic plates, can produce chemical reactions, and can be polarized; that is to say, it can act like lasers in that all its rays can travel in one direction. It is not certain that animals can emit light in polarized form, but there does seem to be the possibility that certain shrimp (*Meganyctiphanes norvegica*) may emit light from its eyes in the form of lasers.

Bioluminescence would seem to represent a vestigial stage in organic evolution, characteristic of bacteria, a form of life that might well have populated primeval seas. These creatures, according to the present view, would have been unicellular, ocean-dwelling organisms, and anaerobic, for whom oxygen would have been lethal. For at that time the atmosphere was composed chiefly of hydrogen and virtually without the free oxygen composing it today. Thus, like bacteria today, they carried on their vital activity through fermentation, living directly off basic chemical elements or rudimentary sugar compounds. Over the course of geologic time, however, the amount of free oxygen in the atmosphere increased, penetrating the ocean, while the hydrogen, being lighter, tended to escape from the earth. Thus, oxygen accumulated below, and the anaerobes could deal with it most effectively by combining it with hydrogen and turning it into water. In the breakdown of a hydrogen compound, enough energy would have been liberated in quanta to excite organic molecules to emit light.

This would explain the fact that all luminous reactions can detect and use oxygen at extremely low concentrations — as bacteria can easily produce measurable light when the oxygen concentration is as low as one part in a hundred million. Subsequently, life forms developed that could use oxygen directly in their metabolism, while those that had developed bioluminescence tended to retain it.

Bioluminescence would therefore seem to be an archaic transformational activity in unicellular metabolism, dependent on an absence of oxygen and the solar radiation so fundamental to later plant and animal life.

If now, we compare the findings of science in regard to bioluminescence with the "phosphorescence" — the "Dark Water" and "Flowing Light" — of our dream, there is a fundamental diversity in the two points of view. Science looks at bioluminescence in terms of its operative principle of causality and cosmic origins. But we have looked at phosphorescence in terms of the subjective aspect of the phenomenon, that is, in terms of the intuitive fantasy images grouped around phosphorescence. We have tried to go beyond the personifying images "Dark Water" and "Flowing Light" and to follow the subjective factor down into the psychoid levels underlying them.

We too have arrived at a cosmological point, as has science; it is a non-solar cosmology, a cosmology representing not so much the birth of consciousness as the birth of psyche. Thus, as we have seen, Steeb's "supercelestial milky water" — a sort of heavenly phosphorescence personified in our dream by "Flowing Light" — is pictured as entering into a *coniunctio* with light, giving birth to the soul of the world, the outpourings of which are absorbed in the "capacious depths of the darksome lower water" [3] — the dark primeval background of the "Dark Water" of our dream, precisely at the point where the phenomenon of bioluminescence is most notable.

It has seemed to me that these two lines of investigation, the extraverted one of science on the one hand and the introverted one of psychology on the other, represent two poles of a single archetype. These two lines converge at this extremely primitive level, characterized by absolute darkness and yet by "atoms" of light of a non-radiant, heatless nature, the "fishes' eyes" of the alchemists. It is a point of absolute unconsciousness, yet with the seeds of consciousness; it can legitimately be considered as shadowing forth a third aspect of the archetype which can be termed psychoid, in that it cannot with certainty be designated either as solely "psychic" or as only "matter."

We have thus approached that aspect of psychic reality which Jung considers in his theory of synchronicity and in his psychological developments from the concept of complementarity in physics. In other words, we are contemplating these phenomena of bioluminescence or phosphorescence as the self-expression of substance, as presentational modes shadowing forth a reality that lends itself to the objective causal formulations of science as well as to the phenomenological organizations of psychology as formulated in the theory of the archetypes. Behind both is the phenomenon of luminosity, the bioluminescence of science converging in the diffuse luminosity of the unconscious as seen in the phenomena studied in depth psychology. Both hint at a transformational activity in substance, in an underlying reality apprehended through symbolic images which, in the human world, creates an imaginal presentation of itself which we call consciousness.

Bioluminescence and phosphorescence would accordingly symbolize an active agency of a cosmological order, shadowing forth a unitary world — the *unus mundus* of the alchemists — not given directly in experience, but ordered according to the archetypal factors and subsisting behind the images through which it presents itself.

CHAPTER V

CORPUS GLORIFICATIONIS:
MOUNT ATHOS AND THE SAPPHIRE FLOOR

"Dark Water" and "Flowing Light" represent regressive aspects of Sol and Luna, and these luminaries in turn represent the symbols for an archetypal consciousness which is projected through the "dark body" of the ego. This projection, carrying with it the transformational activities of the self, has the character of a "cosmogony" or the "creation of the world." As an activity of an archetype of consciousness, this "creation" has two aspects. On the one hand it is timeless and eternal and transpersonal. It constitutes the *a priori* condition for the psyche's experience of consciousness, being the bio-psychic foundation of consciousness in the species and independent of the environment. Yet on the other hand, this archetype, like all archetypes, also has an environmental aspect. It is "evoked," "accumulates experience," and "unfolds" because of the specific environment into which it has been "coded." Hence it not only constitutes the possibility of the psyche's experience, but also constitutes "the world" which the psyche experiences. It not only has a superhuman divine pole which is eternal, spiritual, and the precondition for any experience of consciousness, but it also has a bio-physical temporal pole and appears as a radical "luminosity" and "photosensitivity" coded into the phylogenetic foundations of life. Hence, it is an intrinsic combination of nature, appearing as *unio naturalis* in the activity of the unconscious instinctual life of *bios*, and yet it also moves in *unio mentalis*, in its eternal aspect, as it is "extracted"

128

from the processes of living matter.

In our present case, we are observing the "destruction of a given world," as embodied in the dominance of a solar consciousness, and the "creation of a world," which is also the birth of a new consciousness. This burgeoning of a "new world" is typically feminine in character in that it has a lunar quality and has its origins in the living matter of the psyche; it is a product of *unio naturalis*, and so has an accent different from the creations of a solar masculine consciousness with their accent on *unio mentalis* and illumination from on high. This intimate relation of the feminine in both sexes to matter, to *bios*, nonetheless has a profoundly spiritual orientation, as we shall see in later dreams. And it raises problems of an ethical and moral order going beyond collective consciousness, so that one is led to conjecture that a specifically moral archetype is active in the background of this process of "birth."

This "birth" comes about as the result of compensatory activities in the archetype as manifested in its environmental aspect. It is here that we find processes of destruction and creation most evident in all of their random, instinctual violence. On the other hand, the normative activity of the archetype in aiming at a balance, and the unconscious but purposive nature of its activities appear precisely in the restoration of its temporal environmental aspect to the context of its eternal, non-temporal aspect. This "restoration" constitutes the "extraction of the shadow" of the archetype of consciousness. In alchemical language, this is expressed as the discovery of a "philosophical gold," or as a bath in the supercelestial divine waters of spiritual regeneration. It aims at a *novus mundus*, or a "glorified body." And, as we have suggested, it is a product of the feminine component in both men and women.

129

With the constellation of the *succus vitae* embodied in the figures of "Dark Water" and "Flowing Light," we can see the archetype of consciousness as manifesting itself primarily in its instinctual aspect, as the funded experience of mankind's deepest biological and animal relations with the environment, as an intrinsic combination of nature. This is to say, we see the archetype revealed in its phylogenetic, "temporal" aspect — but "time" seen as a process of "acquiring experience," as a diastasis, as a zoetic drive in the psyche as it moves from one biological stage of life to another.

In this sense, time is the life of the soul. It works as a sort of persistent memory, as a "presence" of the psyche to itself in terms of the juxtaposition of various "psychic positions" or states of itself in its phylogenetic aspect. But if time is the life of the soul, nonetheless it mirrors the eternity which is the life of the archetype in its *a priori* aspect. And it is the tension between these two aspects of the archetype, and the numinosity and fascination uniting them — in alchemical language, the "magnet" — that produces the condition for a "higher consciousness," for a "drive toward spirit," for the symbolic transformation of instinctual biological phenomena into psychic experience which is the deepest aim of *unio mentalis*.

In *A*'s psychology, the constellation of "Dark Water" and "Flowing Light" constituted a conversion or reversal in the very ground-plan of her feminine personality. Henceforth the spiritual orientation predominates, working like a new instinct and creating a new longing. This birth of a new drive toward consciousness is felt as a sort of subterranean convulsion, as an earthquake, as a death and resurrection.

Again, Santa Croce with its connotation of religious conflict becomes the milieu of this process, beginning with two earthquake-dreams. And again the motif of the sacred embassy appears, but this time with the

sacred island of the self as its goal. The Agathodaimon serpent makes
its appearance. And the sequence reaches its termination in the sacred
island of "Mt. Athos" which rests on a floor of sapphire. Here, therefore, "Dark Water" and "Flowing Light" have united in a transfigured
state, as the *lapis*, as the sapphire throne of God, as the divine waters
above the heavens, and as exhibiting the archetype of consciousness
in its eternal and spiritual aspect.

We can follow this development in a series of five dreams which
occurred over a period of two weeks. The first dream goes as follows:

> *A* is in an unknown house in Santa Croce. Something
> extremely important is about to happen. Then there is a
> violent earthquake, and she is bruised on the right flank,
> which becomes a livid purple. Then she is looking for a
> small round box containing something of great value.

On two successive nights there occur these dreams:

> *A* is in an unknown house in Santa Croce with an elderly
> and very wise man. The atmosphere is strange and numinous.
> Then something happens: there is an earthquake and they
> rush out. *A* sees the elderly wise man going along a parallel
> path on the banks of a river carrying something which she
> has forgotten. She feels remorse. She then sees a great
> flower vase of white china, hexagonal in form, belonging to
> her mother.

...and on the following night:

> *A* is in Santa Croce, where she must find food. She
> finds five or seven eggs on a rush mat. Each has a hole in it,
> so that they cannot be eaten. The town is dominated by the
> despotic father of her friend Ludovica (an exaggerated image
> of her own neurosis). This father embarks on a great sailing
> vessel and is borne away by the wind. Then *A* is in a fast

131

galley going to an island. They enter a narrow channel, going against a strong wind and sea. The galley seems to fly over the waves and the spray at the bow makes wings, but the pilot steers very well and they arrive. There *A* finds an altar-retable of myriad colors, of enchanting and noble beauty.

The sequence continues as follows, in which the moral factor appears:

A is on a tram with other women. She is very ill, as are they, and must swallow a living serpent. She then visualizes this serpent upright in her stomach, devouring her illness. It is as though she were looking at an aquarium, in which the morbid fronds of flesh in her stomach are like seaweed which the serpent consumes. Then *A* is on the shores of the sea. A warplane swoops down to strafe the beach, but *A* shoots the pilot. She is then accused of murder by the mob. Only an unknown man helps her, and she finally succeeds in reaching an elderly man of supreme authority. There she is accused of murdering a little girl, the daughter of Ludovica. But the little girl is with her, alive and well; she has lost blood because she is ill. The Judge recognizes *A*'s innocence and she is freed.

The final dream goes thus:

A is with her father and brother approaching an island that they have tried to reach many times before. They pass over a small arm of the sea and land on the shore. The island is called "Mount Athos" because it has a mountain in the center, up the side of which is built a monastery. Her mother dwells on the island as a spiritual presence. After eating with the inhabitants, they leave by an underground gallery. *A*'s father goes ahead, sweeping out the white snow which fills the gallery. He thus reveals the floor of the gallery, which is made of an incredibly beautiful sapphire.

132

I do not propose to analyze these dreams in detail, interesting and rich as they are. Instead, I shall confine myself to their central motifs: the earthquake, the swallowing of the serpent, the accusal and the sacred island with the gallery floored with sapphire.

In general, earthquakes in dreams have a positive significance in that they symbolize a change in the foundations of the personality which manifests itself also in the conscious attitude. Furthermore, there are usually two of them, as Jung points out, [1] one occurring at the moment of the separation of the soul from the body, as at the moment of Christ's death, with its accompanying eclipse, and the second on Easter morning, when the soul is restored to the body. Only then did Christ descend to preach to the souls imprisoned in Hell.

These earthquakes correspond to certain points in a logical sequence of psychological states, although it is important to bear in mind that the sequence is logical and not necessarily encountered empirically in this rigorous order. The earthquakes symbolize two modes of the *coniunctio*. In the first, the *coniunctio* appears as a nefarious marriage, involving incest, murder, or death. It reflects an ego-bound state with a feeble dominant of collective consciousness, frequently symbolized by a sick king about to die. A situation analogous to the solar backdrop of Regine's invocation to the moon has created itself, as appears in Ibsen's *Ghosts*.

There then follows an ascendency of the unconscious and/or a descent of the ego into the unconscious: this is symbolized as a disappearance into the mother's body or as dissolution into water. The "ascendency" of the crab-rock and the rescue of the little black dog reflect this state, as does the bath in the Red Sea. The mother is in the process of dissolving herself in her own substance, to reappear as the anima-daughter.

The second earthquake occurs at a third stage, where a conflict and synthesis of conscious and unconscious occurs. Images of pregnancy, illness, or a display of colors make their appearance, and the corresponding *coniunctio* has a more heavenly character, as appears in the sapphire floor of Mt. Athos. This can appear also in images like the red dress, the livid color of the burns, in motifs of ascent and descent, etc. Sometimes the earthquake motif itself may be "latent," manifesting itself primarily as an emotional tonality.

The sequence terminates in the formation of a new dominant, accompanied by images of the King's Son, the hermaphrodite, or the *rotundum*. In *A*'s psychology, the round box, the blond youth, as well as the parallel feminine and masculine homoeroticisms, are examples.

The earthquake is analogous to an eclipse of the sun by the moon. A dark cloud rises up, obtenebrating consciousness. The widening of consciousness is first experienced as upheaval and darkness: the soul leaves the body after the *coniunctio*. The result is darkness and death: the early fruits of the union appear in images of poisonous reptiles, predators, ill-omened scavengers, birds of prey. The sharks and eels, the dog, the strafing airman, as well as the crabs, leopards and lions of later dreams are examples.

The scene of *A*'s first earthquake is in some way associated with her ancestral village, Santa Croce. Its consequence is to produce a bruise whose livid color recalls the color of her burns and her poisoned hand after the voyage to her mother in Australia. Here, the purple bruise appears on her right side.

The dream pictures a situation analogous to that of Christ's death on the Cross. There is the wounding of Christ by the piercing of the right pleural cavity, in our dream appearing in the livid bruise. This wound has its origin in the "serpent bite," which introduced a deadly sickness into nature through Adam. In *A* we have seen this poison panacea in the serpent-bite in "Australia" with its portentous consequences. A point of "passage" and a manifestation of the self is felt as a wounding and defeat of the ego.

The convulsion of the earthquake brings to the surface a box containing an object of great value which nonetheless must be searched for. Similarly, in the earthquake at the Crucifixion, tombs were split open, and Golgotha — "the place of the skull" — raises memories of the skull of Adam, from which the Cross is pictured as springing. In our dream, the scene transpires in the shadow of Santa Croce, and the round box, like Adam's skull, becomes the "container" at once of death and life.

From the standpoint of our Sol-Luna symbolism, the mercurial union of sea and sky in the dream of the stranded leviathan has produced transformational resonances at an extremely deep level. For in the earthquake a union of Sol as the "black sun in the earth," the "central fire," the burning magma of the core, with Luna in her darkest form as *Physis*, has occurred. This collision between *ignis gehennalis* and the elemental blackness of Earth gives birth to a third being: the round box, the symbol of the *rotundum*, the image at once of completeness and perfection. The hellish fire of black sulphur and earth, uniting in the very ground-plan of the personality, has produced in the wounding an archetypal death experience on the one hand and a promise of redemption on the other.

In our dream, a certain analogy to Christ's Passion is presented also in another way, grouping together the meaning of previous symbols. For the bruise on the right flank, corresponding to the serpent-bite and the piercing of Christ's right pleural cavity, acts rather like a *stigmatum*. Its purple color, associated with the death of the Saviour, the Sacrifice of the Son, and ecclesiastical mourning, appeared after the burning immersion in the *aqua pontica* and after the serpent-bite. Here, however, the *stigmatum* seems to evoke an unconscious prophetic memory, a memory of a resurrection which is hinted at in the necessity for searching for the sacred casket. For if death alone followed, she would not search, and if there were no unconscious memory of the existence of some magic value, she could not search.

The bruised flank caused by the earthquake corresponds, at a higher level, to the puncturing of the ship on the sunken crab-shaped rock.

The religious analogies in this dream, as well as the "sacred missions" which *A* performs and certain ritual gestures in later dreams which underline the numinous importance of otherwise personal or conventional contents, are of the greatest importance, for they point to the correlation of instinct and religion.

Religion, as Jung observes, [2] on the primitive level means the psychic regulatory system that is co-ordinated with the dynamism of instinct. That is, instinct can be formulated in biological and physical terms, but its meaning cannot be exhausted that way. Instincts are also meaningful fantasy structures. The activity of the instinct, its inner pattern, is correlated to a precise *a priori* situation which "triggers" instinct, so that its activity is never "random" but depends on the situation which acts as the symbolic equivalent, the fantasy structure, and releases the genetic pattern in the *soma*. There is accordingly a symbolically oriented aspect to instinct, working toward the transformation of the instinct as a natural drive. The activating situation becomes the "portrait" of the instinct, its "meaning," and the fruition of its vitality. There is thus a selective factor at work, limiting the instinct's unlimited somatic drive to fulfull itself and, in releasing instinctual energy, tending also toward symbolic fulfillment. A process is set in motion in the *soma* which is modified by its own outcome. This selectivity in the constellation of instinctual patterns is reflected also in primitive religious systems, where the unlimited drive of the instinct toward wholeness is set about by a complicated system of rites, taboos and class systems, which work at once selectively and transformationally in relation to instinct.

These limiting and selective factors are reflected in physiological facts, like those which appeared in A's asthma, etc., and also in their translation from physiological phenomena into psychic experience, as well as in the "feminine conscience" which at once holds eros in check and also works for its symbolic transformation. Similarly, "Flowing Light" as an immanent luminosity or "photosensitivity" in the plasm of *bios*, in the "Dark Water" of the *prima materia* of femininity, alludes to such a spiritualizing, reflective factor, which bends instinct around upon itself in accordance with the exigencies of spirit. Such a "bending back" of instinct, such a shift in the center of gravity in the total organism, as it moves out of the level of biological behavior and into the level of psychic experience, is felt as a violent *opus contra naturam*, as an "earthquake" in which subjective life is born as a new reality. In the alchemical *opus* this consists in the creation of a "subtle" or "glorified" body.

At a higher level, the primary interdependence of instinct and religion may be lost, and then, as in the "modern woman," not only eros, but everything going under the name of instinct, like hunger and power drives and sexuality, is disturbed, while on the other hand, a sort of primitive super-ego religion tries to be the antidote to instinct. Here, "prudery" overshadows "*pudor*" and contributes its corruption to the pork, or it causes the poisonous solar constituent in the eros of Regine, or finally, the hydrophobic symptoms of the dog.

This split is not a meaningless catastrophe: it forms part of the evolutionary process itself in extending and differentiating consciousness. There is no energy without a tension of opposites and no consciousness without a perception of differences. Yet an abnormal stretching produces polarity and conflict which, though useful and indeed indispensable for the further development of consciousness, can also prove injurious. The result is that a counter-movement sets in, attempting a reconciliation.

Here we have both the problem and the deeper meaning of the "modern woman." For just as she produces an intensified polarity which seems very "modern" and raises to consciousness factors which seem "masculine" and which are left out of the dominant masculine view, so too she activates unconscious rites linked to forgotten customs belonging to the primitive state of man whose aim was precisely to reconcile conflicting opposites. These rites are performed by men and women, but their content emanates from the divine sphere which is past, present and future. These rites therefore unite the instinctual pattern or pole of the constellated archetype to its divine, spiritual pole: the animal shadow of the archetype and its superhuman, divine aspect are linked together. A "reversal" occurs, in which the shadow of a latent consciousness at a psychoid level is extracted and "sublimated." The archetype in its archaic aspect is raised to a contemporary level. This represents the "foreshortening," the contraction along the linear axis of a given content, appearing in dream sequences. The various animus images terminating in "Flowing Light" represent such a foreshortening.

A's "embassies" and ritual gestures constitute spontaneous anamneses of a religious nature, anamneses of ancestors which are the equivalents of ancestral interventions. *A*'s "berserker" episodes are an example of such "memories." They are actions belonging to an age of ancestral heroes, where a situation of distress was relieved by divine intervention constellated in ritual, and they extend even further backward to a prehistoric world of totemic ancestors. Their aim, in Jung's view, is to constellate the archetype of Man, *Anthropos*, the essential core of great religions, where the heights and depths of creation are reunited in the image of the *homo maximus*.

This deeper meaning of *A*'s dreams — especially those involving Santa Croce — and the state of distress which they seek to alleviate explain in great part the contents which appear. Mankind, either through stupidity or sin, that is, through unconsciousness or through the malignity of a God reflected in the state of possession by a dominant conscious attitude, has forgotten its origination in an archetypal ancestor. Hence the situation of distress which triggers the religious instinct — the instinct to wholeness.

Frequently, too, this instinct to wholeness appears in regressive form, as an "instinct to unholiness," as in the eschatological regression in the Palestine dream. There pride and concupiscence hark back to a stage when hunger, rather than sex or power, was the primary expression of the religious instinct. Thus a tabooed food must be eaten or a serpent swallowed, constellating ritual practices whose deepest meaning collides violently with the contemporary attitude, and in colliding, works for its destruction and transformation. The activation of this instinct appears in *A*'s compulsive eating and vomiting, and its symbolic nucleus appears, as we have seen, in the rotted pork, which constitutes a sort of pregnancy diet for Queen Luna.

We thus have allusions to a state of weakness and disintegration of an ego-attitude, a state in which the "Father" dies in the person of the

"Son," as we saw it in the Palestine dream with the "accidental" murder of the son, or as appears in the death of Oswald in *Ghosts*. There then followed the "ascendence of the unconscious" in the form of the submerged rock — a sort of submarine mountain on which the ship was wounded — and the ship's subsequent "dissolution in the water" after *A*'s sacred embassy had been accomplished. Subsequently, however, this rock, this crab-shaped "submarine mountain," is transformed. In a sort of submarine cosmogony, it emerges from the sea and becomes, first, the island with the many-colored altar, and then finally "Mount Athos," while the sea in which it had its origin is preserved, transformed, in the sapphire floor of the gallery, which becomes a sort of firmament placed over the abyss of *prima materia*. It represents, in fact, the transmuted, spiritualized union of "Dark Water" and "Flowing Light."

These ulterior evolutions are foreshadowed in the second earthquake, and this second earthquake, in turn, appears as the value, latent as it were, in the sacred box. A violent change in the conscious attitude occurs. A new and important father-image appears for the first time. In some obscure way, he is connected with the terrestrial convulsion, and he is seen at the end of the dream as following a separate path, carrying something "that *A* has forgotten." In effect, a splitting up of her identification with the father has taken place. He carries a psychic burden which belongs to him, and *A*'s "forgetfulness" and "remorse" I think here mean her liberation from a compulsive burden which has obsessed her mind. She has been allowed "to forget" an obsessive mode of behavior, and she has been allowed to "remember" something as a result of this liberation: precisely, "remorse" for the distortion which a compulsive identification has worked on the father-image, as well as remorse for her seduction by the father, with the consequent loss of a moral orientation proper to her feminine conscience.

Remorse, like *pudor*, accordingly alludes to a nascent moral insight, for it expresses at once the necessity of a sin as a psychological experience and the regret that only through this necessary sin can its moral nature be recognized. It is, so to speak, a sin without guilt.

For this reason, in the Old Testament Yahveh is pictured as feeling remorse, or as "bethinking himself" of something which he has "forgotten." Remorse, forgetting, remembering, like sacrifice, death and crucifixion, or like the depressional sequence pictured in the "vesperal-matutinal" alternations in the angelic hierarchy and in the Creation in Genesis: all of these picture archetypal happenings, events exhibiting the vitality of the self. Their aim is to stimulate reflection and an enlargement of consciousness, and they have their origin in the transhuman sphere, in the God-image which, empirically, is indistinguishable from the self.

These considerations suggest an important characteristic in the psychology represented by the "modern woman." For just as her animus possession seems limited to relatively superficial layers of her mind, so too the father-image in her personality has attributes in his depths which render him something more than an animus image. He becomes the carrier of the archetype of spirit, both negative and positive, in an eminent degree. And while this is peculiarly evident in his "cosmological" antecedents, as "wind" or as "Flowing Light," so too the wisdom he represents has a lunar saline character — as appears in *A*'s physiological disturbances, in her symptomatology, in her suffering, "remorse" and *"pudor"* — which makes him more nearly a personification of the self than an animus figure. In the "modern woman," therefore, the self can appear with accentuated masculine characteristics, and these find expression not only as "possession" but also as the deepest aim of her individuality, in which a striving after a new and enriching capacity for moral awareness is discernible. Alchemically speaking, white sulphur is the active agency in these phenomena.

In the light of these observations, the paradoxical "forgetting" and "remembering" in our dream seems to express events in the self, appearing with the violence of an earthquake, rather than phenomena associated solely with the ego's psychology. They are events transpiring in the "dark body of the ego," the ego considered as a personification of the self, and not in the ego in its waking, empirical diurnal state.

The "forgetting" and "remembering" are symbolic, therefore, and constitute a sort of death and resurrection. In the unconscious there has occurred a shadowy and unseizable "mystical" experience, not unusual in introverted aspects of the sensation function, leading to a sort of indescribable broadening out toward wholeness, toward archetypal Man. In alchemical symbolism, the "waters of fructifying interest" now point upward: the *novilunium* becomes a *plenilunium*, and the "dog" is transformed into a volatile, spiritual energy that can look at the sun.

This means that in the depths, in the "Dark Water" of *A*'s feminine nature, a profound change has occurred, and this is correlated to a change in the masculine image, in "Flowing Light." Her eye, which before saw only dangers and wretchedness now turns toward the full moon, corresponding to the fullness of her feminine consciousness; the spirit moving within the "waters over the abyss" has worked this transformation.

The earthquakes accordingly picture a situation in which not only the ego suffers a shock from the activation of the unconscious, but some of the light of consciousness penetrates into the unconscious, so that it is not so remote. This "illumination" of the unconscious

142

does not mean that it is any less unconscious, but its contents pass over into consciousness more easily than before and its imagery henceforth gradually takes on a more acceptable form. Each of the events and transformations in *A*'s dreams which we have noticed depends on an inner working of Mercurius, each represents a state in the reconstruction of *Anthropos*, the divine archetypal image of Man, and each of these steps signifies a rebirth of Deity.

The images of illness and conflict as well as synthesis of consciousness and the unconscious which herald the second earthquake now appear in positive form.

The vision of the white flower vase of her mother points to a state of *albedo*, of readiness for a "flowering" of her femininity, and for the reception of a fertilizing "water" analogous to that in the *lacrimariae*. The six sides of the vase express a state of expectancy, of awaited fulfillment; it hints at *coniunctio* and pregnancy.

The appearance of the hexagonal vase after the earthquake, the "forgetting and remembering," and the "remorse," is of the greatest interest. On the one hand it alludes to the breaking up of the shadow-animus identification which has been the curse of *A*'s neurosis. And on the other hand it points toward the "birth of the soul" — the reunion of *unio mentalis* to a transformed "subtle" or "glorified" body — and to the creation of a "new world" appropriate to the nascent psychic state. Finally, it alludes to the elevation of the phosphorescent "Flowing Light" and "Dark Water" of a primeval Aphrodite to a higher, "celestial" level of being.

These possibilities can be deduced from the alchemist Johannes Lydus' observations on the number six. [3] For, as he points out, six means the "sixth day" and is ascribed to Phosphorus the morning

143

star, which precedes the rising of the day-star, the sun. Phosphorus is the begetter of warmth and generative moisture; he is, perhaps, the son of Aphrodite, as is Hesperis, the evening star. Aphrodite herself is the nature of the visible universe, the first-born Hyle, which the oracle names star-like as well as heavenly.

Six is at once even and uneven, active and passive, hylical and spiritual, symbolizing completeness and perfection. The ancients called it "marriage" and "harmony," so that it is both male and female, like Aphrodite herself, who is hermaphroditic.

Six is soul-producing and belongs to the "psychogonia": it multiplies itself into the world sphere and in it the opposites are intermingled. It leads, Lydus concludes, to like-mindedness and friendship, giving health to the body, harmony to music, virtue to the soul, prosperity to the state and forethought to the universe.

Psychologically, the double triad forming the vase illustrates the impact of a coagulating and differentiating process on the total psyche as the container, as a container which is in process of transformation from states of unconscious identity and physiological reactions into the realm of the psyche as such. It is this that constitutes the "soul-making," the "psychogonia"; the atmosphere is one of expectancy, of awaited fulfillment, symbolized by the flower vase.

This expectation has been realized in the following dream. The five or seven eggs have hatched out. The holes here, as in the *lacrimariae*, mean transcendence: spirit has given birth to winged beings which are the spiritual aspect of the feminine. The negative "father of the neurosis" is borne away on the wind, while *A* again goes on a sacred embassy and after encountering the wind and high seas of the strait, – a "bipontic" situation – finds the many-colored altar on the island. The images

144

of pregnancy and the display of colors – the *cauda pavonis* – associated with the second earthquake have been realized, hinting at a heavenly *coniunctio* and an imminent rebirth. The *rotundum* has appeared in the form of the eggs and is repeated in the circular shape of the island.

The imagery of this dream – of the island with the many-colored altar – is reminiscent of that of the Gnostic Sethians picturing the union of a spiritual masculine principle and a feminine psychic principle. In it the conjunction, "the tryst of wind and water" in the waves of the strait, like that in the dream of the stranded leviathan, again appears.

> But when this wave is raised from the water by the wind* and made pregnant in its nature and has received within itself the reproductive power of the feminine, it retains the light scattered from on high together with the fragrance of spirit, and that is Nous, given shape in various forms. This [light] is a perfect God who is brought down from the unbegotten light on high and from the spirit, into man's nature as into a temple, by the power of nature and the movement of the wind. It is engendered from the water and commingled and mixed with the bodies as if it were the salt of all created things, and a light of the darkness struggling to be freed from the bodies, and not able to find a way out. For some very small spark of light is mingled with the fragrance from above... Therefore every thought and care of the light from above is how... Nous may be delivered from the death of the sinful and dark body, from the father below, who is the wind which raised up the waves in tumult and terror, and begot Nous, his own perfect son, who is yet not his own son in substance. For the son was a ray of light from on high, from that perfect light overpow-

---

* That is, by *pneuma*, by the Holy Spirit.

ered in the dark and terrible, bitter polluted water, and
a striving spirit carried away over the water...[4]

In this impressive passage we can see the central operative images
which appeared in Johann Steeb's references to the "milky waters"
above: the *coniunctio* with light and the chlorophyll — the "blessed
greenness" — as motive agencies in the *anima mundi*. Here, however,
the images are more "mythological," tending toward personification
and hence toward integration at a human level, even if that humanity
remains itself archetypal.

In our dream, the tyrant-father sailing away in the sailing ship and
the "Father below" show a certain mysterious affinity; he is the
Demiurge, at once the "begetter of life" and the "begetter of death."
The hatched-out eggs suggest how the reproductive power of the
feminine has been activated, giving birth to winged spirit — retaining
the "light scattered from on high and fragrance of spirit" and giving
"shape to Nous in various forms," as the many-colored altar shows.
This entry of the light and spirit from on high "into man's nature, as
into a temple" appears as the island with its central altar — an image
of the self as a sacred island. The tumultuous waves, the power of
nature and the movement of the wind, demonstrate the power of the
"Father below."

This Father begets a Nous-son who is yet not identical to himself
but hints at a transformative power in which he too participates. The
unbegotten light-son "from on high" reveals perfections which the
"Father below" has lost, for this Son illuminates, from "within,"
the "dark and terrible, bitter polluted water" into which spirit has
been absorbed and in which light-Nous goes on living in the form of
a serpent.

This "Light Son" from on high, mixed into the "terrible, bitter polluted water," thus repeats the psychic situation symbolized by "Dark Water" and "Flowing Light." The "light" from on high becomes, as it were, a sort of bioluminescent "salt" — "a very small spark of light" mingled in the pneumatic "fragrance from on high," carrying with it not only the astringent bitterness of salt, but also its wisdom and its resonances giving rise to feelings of moral redemption.

A, in her masculine aspect, thus becomes a "son," akin to the "Father below" but of a "different substance" — different precisely because of the heavenly origins of the luminous phosphorescence immanent in her lunar nature. *A*'s "son-ship," akin to but of a different nature from a chthonic masculinity, means a type of illuminative insight and consciousness which is not reducible to biological sexual differences and which supplements the "cold light" of the ithyphallic Hermes with the "warm light" extracted from the Negro youth of Piazza San Silvestro.

Thus a fundamental *coniunctio* and differentiation has occurred in which *A*'s "heroic" role of animus daughter has moved out of the infected eros of *Ghosts*, out of the sinister chthonic level of incest, and has been revealed as a "new son-ship" of spirit — a spirit misapprehended in collective consciousness but representing her true destiny as a "modern woman."

———

The preceding dreams with the earthquake motif, the wounding, the appearance of a positive father who carries something that *A* has "forgotten and remembered," the nascent moral element of "remorse," and the background hint of a "new son-ship" lead into the serpent dream, with its ambiguous accusal, first of the murder of the airman, then of child-murder. Here *mercurius menstrualis* appears in the blood motif, which is at first construed as evidence of child-murder until the presence of the child herself contradicts this. The blood is then seen as evidence of illness, and here too, like the Negro in the San Silvestra dream, an unknown man helps *A* and she is absolved by a wise judge. As in other dreams which we have examined, we shall find certain Gnostic images of the greatest help in opening up the deeper processes in the patient's unconscious.

In this dream the whole moral problem becomes explicit. The serpent, the airman, the child, the blood and the Wise Old Man enter into a complex system of polarities, posing and resolving a moral question going beyond convention. Collective opinion condemns her at first for the murder of the aggressive airman. Her crime appears as a social one, that of refusing an identification with an aggressive libido. This represents an advance over her "murder of the son" in the Palestine dream. Yet, at this point, a curious change takes place. For now the murder appears as child-murder, as a crime against her femininity. Collective opinion sees her only in the role of Hecate or Medea. Yet this accusation is false.

A has thus acted as the *scintilla*, the igniting spark, in this situation. She has precipitated a tension in which, in the dream, moral judgments are made which not only her waking ego has omitted to make, but which collective consciousness itself has not perceived. One suspects, therefore, that this constitutes an essential aspect of her "new son-ship"; it aims at developing a type of consciousness that perceives an ethical factor in a situation which goes beyond penal codes based on "crime" and "punishment" and which cannot be explained as a regression to a "Medea complex." Indeed, the nascent type of consciousness hinted at in this dream looks beyond the ailing child, the "pathology" of the situation, in search of a still unknown meaning having a moral and ethical quality that expresses a fundamental finality, an eschatology, moving in the whole process.

Here the judgments and the absolution seem to transpire from "beyond" the ego-figure and the other personages in the dream. *A* is only the "carrier" of the problem — she is only one among many women who must "swallow the serpent." She precipitates the intervention of spirit somewhat as we saw in the "dare" of the bipontic dream and in the "accident" of the Palestine dream, but with the difference that her action here is purposive, yet enigmatic. The motivations of the ethical judgments still remain obscure. There is an "uncertainty factor" that matches the shifting substance of accusal, from a crime against aggressive masculine spirit to a blood crime against her growing femininity. This latter accusal is in itself extremely ambiguous. For the "symptom" of the illness of the child looks like murder to public opinion: it is a "pathology" that has the qualities of a crime, as far as the chorus of this drama is concerned.

Illness and death by violence are associated, but here "pathology" seems a justification and brings absolution. Yet the moral issue still remains: crime may come of illness, yet illness may also be a crime. The most we can say at this point is that a problem of ethical value is involved going beyond concepts of blame, guilt and punishment. Paradoxically, it is as though there were a "sin without guilt" involved in this situation, which is essential to a factor hidden in the drama pictured by the dream. *A*'s "new son-ship" is the sparking element pointing toward this hidden factor. Perhaps embedded in this "pathology" and apparent child-murder there is a hidden sacrificial archetype: a sacrifice exempt from more or less manifest ego-claims for averting evil or invoking good from the divine; a sacrifice whose aim is simply to attune one to autonomous transpersonal processes, to destinies having a hidden

149

ethical finality.

From this point of view, it seems to me that we must conjecture a fundamental creative process at work, emanating from an archetype of value which is still in a state of latent consciousness and latent projection, i.e., a state of total unconsciousness, such as the Gnostics described as emanating from a "blessed, non-existent God." In our dream, the blood acts as a *succus vitae* focusing our attention on this genuinely unconscious content. But the helpful unknown man likewise has a mercurial function. He relates *A* to the judge, but he also probably represents an aspect of the airman which has been extracted through *A*'s action. Finally, the judge himself is very enigmatic. He absolves *A* from a crime that has *not* been committed, although the preceding conflict with the airman did involve a death and a crime that remains unclarified.

The judge functions, therefore, but he keeps his thoughts to himself. It is as though he is aware that there is evil in the parents that can only come to light in their offspring — hence the absolution from an uncommitted crime. He acts less like a super-ego than as the personification of a center of insight which is only formally involved with the events pictured in the dream. It is as though his real interest were within, looking beyond the crime and illness, beyond pathology and therapy. Thus, he too acts like a *succus vitae*, focusing attention on a deeply buried unconscious content, and his enigmatic behavior leads us to return again to that paradox of "sin without guilt." In the preceding part of the dream a sort of situational morality has been pictured, in which "blame" or accusal, "guilt" and "punishment" are split apart and, as it were, obsessionally related to each other. But if the projected elements of a moral act are withdrawn and interiorized, one could say that a maximum state of ethical consciousness would be achieved precisely in the perception of a state of sin, but without punishment, guilt, accusal, etc. In such a state of intense moral awareness, the evil which is a component of the universe begins to acquire moral identity and present itself as a moral and ethical problem of consciousness itself.

The judge seems to exhibit a type of consciousness that is moral and ethical, that is oriented inward, that looks beyond the situational polarities of morality to evil itself as a meaningful component of the universe, a component that is transpersonal, and even, we might say, transpsychological. A sort of "third cosmology" seems to be going on in the background of the dream, following on the "natural cosmology" of *unio naturalis* and the psychological cosmology of *unio mentalis*. It involves the "forethought in the universe," as Lydus put it, but its content is still hidden in the cosmological quality of the psyche's unknown essence, an essence that is the subjective correlate to objective energetic processes uniting both spirit and matter. Alchemically speaking, white sulphur would seem to be the active agency moving in the serpent: in A; in the airman, the accusal, the blood; in the judge, who is the enigmatic agent of this emergent archetype of value.

The ingested serpent represents this new development, appearing at once as a fertilizing agency and as a content in A's personality. It constitutes a sort of "pregnancy diet," and is nourished, like a fetus, by the diet. The hero — the embryonic new sun of consciousness — is being nourished in his hermetic snake-form in the "dark waters" and "flesh" of A's lunar aspect. It is being incubated and, as it were, sublimated. Thus, the unconscious is pregnant with consciousness and gives birth to it.

This *"cibatio"* has something of the character of a totem-meal in which the king was devoured for the good of the race. It harks back to a state of mind where youthful dying Gods are dismembered, eaten, mourned — Gods like Tammuz, Adonis, Dionysus, Osiris, as well as Christ. The serpent-form of the hero can also appear as a cult phallus, as after the dismemberment of Osiris, whereby a ritual "spiritual" and anti-natural "fertilization" of the Isis-priestess is worked. This mythologem appears in a later dream, where *A* sees a dark woman being violated by a wooden phallus moved by invisible spirits. This dream, incidentally, coincided with the remission of her homoerotic fantasies.

In our present dream, the serpent has not only been "devoured" as a "pregnancy diet" but is being "fed" by the morbid illness which is thus cured. Psychologically, this means that the "sick king of consciousness" is being fed not only by the darkness of the animal sphere, but also by an animal spirit. As Jung says, animal symbols point upward and downward at the same time [5] — hence the vertical position of the serpent, whose function here is not, strictly speaking, uroboric. Consciousness is being enriched by the unconscious through an inner participation in a conflict between a chthonic and a spiritual nature. This presents a moral problem which, as in our dream, frequently transcends convention, and in which failure to know what one is doing acts like guilt and is paid for as dearly.

These considerations open onto more complex problems involved in the serpent symbol. Although we cannot treat them here in their full complexity, nonetheless, certain observations on the chthonic and spiritual aspects of the serpent may be helpful.

In the first place, the serpent corresponds to the shadow for most people. It constellates not only the region of the personal unconscious but also the collective unconscious, which stretches down, as we have seen, from the collective historical deposits of man's past experience to the animal soul of man, and thence to the cold-blooded reptilian and fish-like strata in man's genetic ancestry, and finally, to the psychoid

152

processes of the sympathetic nervous system. Here one not only meets the animal psyche in man but also the anima-character as psychopomp in both sexes. The snake, like the fish, corresponds to deep levels of the unconscious, which are correlated to physiological and organic symptoms as expressions of psychic disorders. The Gnostics identified the serpent with the medulla and spinal cord — synonyms for reflex actions. This level we have seen active in *A*'s asthma, in the "poison," as well as in the "phosphorescence" which gave birth to "Flowing Light."

Secondly, the snake represents the lowest level of the psyche. It symbolizes evil and darkness, unrelatedness, ruthless instinct oblivious of morality, opening onto levels which are totally unconscious and incapable of becoming conscious. Yet, as the collective unconscious and as instinct, it symbolizes a peculiar knowledge and wisdom of its own. This is the treasure which the snake guards, and that is why it signifies darkness and evil and poison on the one hand and wisdom on the other. The serpent represents the greatest tension of opposites. This polarity is so great that to St. Augustine it seemed as though sin itself must be a divine intervention, correlated to saving grace. Hence the paradoxical correlation of the serpent and fish with the Christ-symbol: on the one hand it symbolized supreme spirituality leading from the *lapis*, to Naas the serpent, to the Nous, Logos, Christ and the Higher Adam, to the *salvator, servator, deus terrenus,* and the Self; and yet on the other hand to the Lower Adam, where the nadir is constellated, the level of the cold-blooded vertebrates and the end of psychic rapport.

Jung has given an extended interpretation of the relation of the serpent- and fish-symbols to Christ in *Aion*. The fish-symbol does not enter into the limits of our present material, yet it appears in later dreams — notably in certain ritual actions in which a small lion attacks or is attacked by sea crabs, where crabs are reduced to a pulp and eaten in the form of a fish, and finally, where *A* buys at the market as a gift for her father a large tuna fish from whose mouth a smaller fish is emerging like a *logos*. Logos-motifs, *prima materia*, disintegration and "pulpification" motifs, and "nourishment" motifs carry on the process outlined here.

In our dream, the serpent is not only a variant of the poisonous eels and sharks in the Australia dream, it is also the *prima materia*, a variation of the rotted pork; in addition it is a mercurial principle. It is the serpent of Hermes or Agathodaimon, now freed of its poisonous aspects. It is the Nous animating the cold, lunar part of nature and should lead to the transformation of the feminine element into the Queen, as the kingly substance is transformed from a lion into Rex.

Hence, the serpent, like salt, has its wisdom. "It is the wise word of Eve," [6] the mystery of the river of Paradise, the sign that protected Cain so that no one should kill him, for the God of this world had not accepted his offering. He moves in Cain, whose name means "possession," and in Abel, whose name means "grief." And he moves in the "new seed" appointed to Eve in place of Abel, from which Seth — whose name means "hope" — was born.

The problem is how to lead this serpentine Nous of darkness — the *serpens mercuriales* — through the stages of transformation: through "sulphur," "salt," "lion" and "rabid dog," through the winged beings like "eagle" and "vulture," to the "Father of all perfection" who stands in contrast to the "Father below" — the "prince of this world" — whom we have seen as the Tyrant Demiurge.

Here again our dreams contain ancient symbolic images. Just as "Dark Water" and "Flowing Light" enabled us to gain an insight into psychoid processes going on in the physiological psyche, so here a similar insight becomes possible. But whereas before the process was descensional, oriented toward *Physis*, here the process is ascensional, aiming at spirit, aiming at restoring the divine Light Nous to the superhuman God on high.

This appears in the inscription in the Temple of Hathor, where the falcon-sun Hathor rises up from a sapphire-colored lotus temple, born from a chthonic serpent.

> The sun, who has existed from the beginning, rises up like a falcon out of the midst of his lotus-bud. When the doors of his petals open in sapphire-coloured splendour, he has sundered the night from day. Thou risest up like the sacred snake as a living spirit... The Divine Lord... multiplies himself a millionfold when the light goes forth from him in the form of a child.[7]

Thus, if in one sense the winged sun is the offspring of the serpent and reveals it, so in another sense the serpent and son are identical, and no one can be saved without the logos-Son in his serpent-form.

"For this (son) is the serpent," says the doctrine of the Paretic Gnostics. "For it is he who brought the signs of the Father [*patrikoi characteres*] down from above." It is the serpent Nous as Son who communicates the "signs of the Father" — the astrological "character" imprinted on the individual by the archons — the chronometric expression of individuality.

> And it is he who carries [the signs of the Father] back again after they have been wakened from sleep... He transfers them to those whose eyelids are closed... as the lodestone draws iron. This, they say, is the perfect race of men, made in the image of the Father: ...drawn from the world by the Serpent, even as it was sent down by him.[8]

We have seen this situation hinted at in the dream of the earthquakes. There, as we noted, a new Father-image emerged, carrying a burden which *A* had forgotten and for which she felt remorse. This corresponds to the "signs of the Father" being "carried back" after *A* has "been wakened from sleep." And he draws forth "the image of the perfect race of men, made in the image and substance of the Father," drawing forth as Serpent, from the world, those archetypal characteristics of the perfect man "from those whose eyelids are closed," that is to say, from one who is about to be reborn. Hence the paradoxical "forgetting" and "remembering" which we noted in reference to these dreams. A deeper memory of oneself is awakened as the result of a "forgetfulness" of one's limited ego-centered personality with its neurotic limitation of vision and its sinful unconsciousness. The Serpent-Son, in the form of contrasting Father-images, of a lost but remembered box, of a forgotten burden, of remorse, of an ingested serpent, and of a "son, akin, but of diverse substance," moves in the background of the earthquakes which have awakened the personality to a new awareness, an awareness elucidated in the subsequent dreams where the myriad forms and colors of the Logos-Serpent-Sun manifest themselves. Thus "salt" has elaborated itself into wisdom, the union of thought and feeling.

We can now see how the mythological background of these dreams prepares for *A*'s serpent dream, with its paradoxical crime and accusal and absolution. Somewhat like Eve in a celebrated encounter with a serpent, *A* stumbles on a problem requiring a moral solution. Her "remorse" is the harbinger of this insight. And this moral solution centers precisely on a feminine conscience which is illuminated by the Wise Man. Her murder of the airman means that she, as a wingless dragon, has slain the winged dragon sent against her by the Tyrant

Father. In some way, this crime of identification with a chthonic power is construed as a crime against the "child-daughter" of her neurotic femininity. Only as a result of the intervention of an unknown man does she reach the Wise Judge and by the presence of the child prove her innocence.

Nonetheless, the "child of her neurosis" is in some way essential to herself; it hints at a development of her own feminine nature to which the illness is fundamental. For if her neurosis has in one sense followed from an illegitimate appropriation of a masculine attitude, on the other hand it is the young and growing part of her femininity which could only live through the death of her identification with the winged dragon. In this way, the illness at once nourishes the serpent and is consumed by it, and the "signs of the father" with which she had identified in her neurotic poisoned state of ego-centered unconsciousness are "carried back to the Father" on a parallel path beside the river, which symbolizes life.

And so, a new growth of moral insight is in process of development, leading to a new reflection on her character, symbolized by the childlike aspect of herself. She has sinned, and yet, in a mysterious way, that sin, in the form of the child, turns out to be also an absolution and a sign of grace. It is, as we have suggested, a paradox, a "sin without guilt." Hence it moves out of the range of a compulsive morality of guilt, blame and punishment.

A new "character," still in an unconscious child-like state, and a new Father, whose "sign" she now bears, have been constellated. The "wound" of the serpent-bite, the *stigmatum*, has worked as a transformational power in the very ground-plan of her identity, for it unites the dark aspect of Luna, who wounds, to the *sponsus* who is wounded. Luna disintegrates him in the evil of the sublunary world, dissolving him

157

in the "dark waters" anterior to the second day of Creation, and yet also this very *solutio* constitutes a *coniunctio*. It activates the "flowing light" immanent in *A*'s primordial femininity and opens the way to the "new son-ship," a son-Nous which is not reducible to the biological sexual differences of men and woman.

———

Some hint of how this will work out is given in the last dream of our series. There the magic island appears for the last time. The sacred mountain of the Mother is joined up its flank by the masculine conventual house of the spirit. *A* with her brother and her father (who makes his first appearance in this dream) reach it — after many previous failures — over an arm of the sea. They commune with the inhabitants and in their communion recapitulate the *coniunctio* of the feminine and masculine spirit overshadowing them. They leave by a journey under the Earth, and the father clears away the snow — the frigidity and bitterness which, in his negative contrasexual aspect, he has caused. In so doing, he reveals the sapphire floor of the gallery, and it is on this symbol that I should like to dwell for a moment.

The sapphire color we have already seen in the "lotus temple," in which the chthonic serpent gives birth to the Sun-Falcon, Hathor, as a child. In the sapphire floor the chthonic serpent is reduced to the *lapis*, and the coldness of his salt-spirit is crystallized into the snow flakes which are swept away by the father. The heavenly nature of this serpent-*lapis* is emphasized by its deep blue color. It becomes a firmament on which both the feminine mountain and the conventual masculine spirit rest. Like the firmament in Genesis, it divides the upper from the lower waters. As "*lapis*" it is the foundation of the whole world, the foundation of the world cast by God into the abyss. It becomes the central point of the world, its axis, upon which stands the Holy of Holies. Through it one can look, *de profundis*, at once into the abyss of Hell and into the power of the saints who, through the inhabitation of the Holy Spirit, have the power to look into the deep things of God. It unites the powers of the upper and lower world and fulfills the function of Adam Kadmon as capital stone. It is called "sapphire" because it takes on diverse colors from the highest celestial powers and works diversely in created things, administering good, evil, life and death, healing and sickness, riches and poverty. It is the power of fate and even of God himself. The sapphire is made of that liquid in which there is no harmful matter; it is the firmament above the living creature, like a "terrible crystal" and "sapphire stone." It is a likeness of the throne of God, as in Ezekiel's vision (1:22 & 26). Exodus 24:10, moreover, says, "And they saw the God of Israel: and under his feet as it were a work of sapphire stone and as the heaven, when clear."

The alchemists remark on the appearance of this ardently desired blue color in the *opus*. For, as they say, it does not darken or dull the eyes as does the splendor of the external sun. Its healing power is gentle and strengthens and sharpens the eyes. This sapphire floor thus represents the *quinta essentia*, the *anima mundi*, the manifestation of divinity in the foundation of God's creation. It represents the fundamental transformation of "Australia" and the poison which *A* found there. "Dark Water" and "Flowing Light" thus reach a spiritual transformation in this image of the celestial *lapis*.

With this great image, therefore, we come to the end of the initial phase of our analysis. The sacred journeys, beginning in the voyages "down under" to Australia; the "abyss" containing the poison cure; the reconstruction of Adam's name in the beginning initials of the continents with their four directions and four co-ordinated elements; the ingestion of the serpent with all that it implies of upper and lower aspects of the psyche — these have led us to this central image of the self and have established a first stage for the reconstruction of the archetype of man.

⸻

By way of conclusion, I would like to attempt a summing up of our investigation. The material presented here appeared during the first five weeks of analysis. If we take the "formula diagram" in *Aion* as a schematic paradigm, the material represents a passage through the psychic positions of the first "counter-clockwise" node. During this period the physiological symptoms vanished, the frigidity showed signs of modification, and somewhat later the homosexual fantasies disappeared, following on a dream in which an ancient Goddess was fertilized "anti-naturally" by an invisible spirit. Analysis continued for another two years. The material forthcoming was always "deep"; there was great improvement in the ego-tone, but extremely deep and difficult problems remained. One might be inclined to suspect psychotic processes from the nature of the material, nor would I exclude this as a possibility. But such a suspicion would not be justified by any failure of adequate reactions to the material or to any lack of insight. Indeed, the patient's deepened insight into the nature of her problem and the courage with which she bore it were notable features of the analysis.

In fact, it seems to me that here we are dealing with problems belonging to the "psychology of the contents" rather than to the "psychology of the person." We are dealing with archetypal processes going beyond "therapy," which is always more or less conditioned by adaptation to "things as they are" and so tends to remain inexorably personalistic, reductive and ego-centered.

Yet, if we look more deeply into the "predominance of the shadow" and the "contrasexual consciousness" of the patient, we see processes moving at a transpersonal level, having to do with the renewal of the anima character of the feminine and the elucidation of a masculine agency in the total personality. Both of these factors have been revealed as going far beyond the usual meanings of anima and animus. They appear, instead, as polar components in a single archetype of consciousness, and through the alchemical paradigm we have been able to study them at a non-personal and, as it were, at a pre-figurative level. This has permitted us to gain some insight into the psychoid level of archetypal activity, both in terms of the bio-genetic life of matter and the transpersonal life of spirit. In other words, in approaching closer to the transcendent "core" of the archetype, we have also approached what might be called the autonomous "psychology of the contents" expressing archetypal activity. We have thus been dealing to a marked degree with a level of the archetype which can *not* be integrated, and which belongs to the processes of the arcane substance of the subjective factor itself.

This accounts for the "cosmological" and religious nature of the material. Psychologically speaking, these phenomena would seem to have their neurological basis in the sympathetic nervous system, and functionally, to exhibit the activities of introverted sensation — a function of inner reality which has been somewhat neglected in analytical writings. Here we see it expressing activities at the psychoid level of the organism.

In this connection I would like to say a word about the Gnostic texts which we have used to elaborate certain dreams. Like alchemy, they have been useful as paradigms for characteristic forms of projection, and so they have given us keys for certain images in the dreams.

161

In addition, they represent the specifically shadow-side of Christian consciousness and are perhaps now coming to light in the evening of the Christian aeon. In addition, Gnosticism is complementary to both the alchemical and astrological systems in that its specific interest was of a religious and moral order, and its images refer to the "eternal" divine pole of the archetype, whereas alchemy's interest extended down into the material pole of the archetype, and astrology pointed toward the chronometric development of cosmic processes in the individual.

We have used these texts as means of gaining insight. This is *not* to assert that these texts have any direct revelance to the dream material in a personal sense. Mt. Athos in the dream and Mt. Athos in reality have no causal connection, and still less does the *Elenchos* of Hippolytus which was discovered at Mt. Athos. Rather, I would be inclined to say that the relation between one of our dream motifs and an image from a Gnostic text is synchronistic: it is an archetypal constellation, non-causally related, but carrying a meaning which is not only by its very nature symbolic but also a *mysterium*, still unknown as far as its specific content is concerned. Hence, the more we seek to approach the core of archetypal meaning, the more we are constrained to the realm of conjecture, to look *per speculum in aenigmate*. This must be borne constantly in mind.

In addition, insofar as we approach the psychoid aspects of an archetype, we are also approaching a realm of "death" as far as human experience is concerned. For an archetype is sometimes said to "die" when its presenting images de-personalize, when they recede "outside the body" into empty space or into totally unrelatable forms of life. This realm of "death" is the archetype's most dangerous aspect; yet, as we have seen, in this transpersonal and even transpsychological sphere we find the deepest, most unchanging, and most creative vitality of the archetype. Men and women are the carriers of these energies, as they are the carriers, genetically and psychologically, of both masculine and feminine components.

Furthermore, in dealing with contents at the psychoid level, it has seemed to me that the "sexual" aspect of the *coniunctio*, like the sexual differentiation of anima and animus, must be taken very symbolically. The sexual aspect of the *coniunctio* is of course pronounced when it appears as an aspect of the transference. But the "transference *coniunctio*" is only one aspect, and by no means the most important, of much deeper archetypal activities. Outside its transference manifestations, the sexuality in the *coniunctio* might better be considered as the vividness, intensity, cohesiveness and autonomous potency of a molecular or chemical combination. At the psychoid level the *coniunctio* seems to have more the cohesive quality of a magnetic field in the subjective factor. In alchemical language this was called the "magnet" — the "lode-stone" in our citation from the Paretic Gnostics, and the "magnet of the Moon" as Paracelsus put it. In antiquity, this "field quality" was seen as a sort of impersonal, non-zonal "vital attention" or inner logos, having all the power of a magnet, focusing the activities of neurobiological processes and tending toward wholeness.

Similarly, one could plausibly argue that at this level anima and animus are pre-sexual in character, factors in the psyche no more necessarily correlated to the biological sex of a person than senex and puer are necessarily correlated to biological age. Anima and animus are poles in a single archetype of consciousness, and although they can be integrated at levels involving a differentiated consciousness appropriate to a masculine or feminine ego, their deeper reaches seem to me to lose this "sexual" quality. They might better be described by the terms *zoe* and *bios*, where *zoe* means the transcendent aspect of life

163

processes and *bios* means the organized forms in which they are realized.

Today we are entering what might be called a new animism. ESP experiments, varied uses of polygraph and EEG techniques, recent studies in bioluminescence, not to mention new departures in the physical and biological sciences that not so long ago remained outside the pale of scientific decency show that we have only the most rudimentary ideas of the ways in which energy, and especially psychic energy, can manifest itself. This "animism" is like the discovery of a world and can perhaps be regarded as a new differentiation of *unio naturalis*, as a creative manifestation through which an emergent experience of psychic reality is coming about. "Matter" is again beginning to show qualities that in ancient times were attributed to divinity.

The Christian aeon sought above all to separate God's substance from his visible manifestations; it represented a long process of *unio mentalis* having a sacramental basis and a moral finality. Perhaps now we are beginning a process of return to a "glorified body" which must be extracted from a redeemed animistic experience of nature. Perhaps this will constitute the *opus* of the new aeon, and, as we have suggested, this would be the fundamental task of the masculine-feminine components in the "modern woman."

If such should prove to be the case, then we are assisting in the creation of a new myth, in a process of soul-making, in a "psychogonia," and the new animism would be the *prima materia* of this process. The Gnostic images have been helpful in reminding us that a mythological process is going on, although it would remain mythological whether or not it is recognized as such. But this process belongs primarily to the procession of the aeons and only secondarily to the individuals who are its carriers.

The masculine and feminine components of this new animism, as it is exhibited by the "modern woman," would aim at a new and more extended consciousness, a consciousness expressing the transformational activities of a central archetype at a psychoid level, at once "eternal" and "genetic," and hinting at a finality going beyond our present day, a process "outside generations," so to speak. And this involves a relativization of the "sexual" nature of our concepts in this regard.

The deepest finality in this process would seem to be of a moral order, matching the cosmogonic way it has been symbolized in our material. The "new son-ship" and the necessary but paradoxical "sin without guilt" seem to point in this direction and to hint at an emergent archetype of value. Here the "dark water" of the modern woman's femininity is aiming at a *novus mundus*, but in a typically feminine way. *Physis* is striving for a "subtle" or a "glorified" body, that is, striving to realize the eternal aspect of the archetype as a specifically psychic reality, a reality that is not reducible to physical or biological causal analogies.

Thus if, like Sophia, she must "fall" and so make matter "visible," on the other hand her "remorse" gives sin its meaning. And so she opens to our view the moral factor, the ethical value moving as the inner essence of consciousness as such. "Dark Water" and "Flowing Light" on the one hand, and the sapphire floor of Mt. Athos on the other, reveal a psychoid process of giving birth to spirit, spirit as a vital inner intensity and as a moral orientation in the most deeply hidden subjective recesses of the psyche.

NOTES

CHAPTER ONE

1. Paracelsus, "De pestilitate" (III, 95), quoted in Jung, *Coll. Wks. 14*, Para. 215.
2. *Ibid.*
3. Jung, *Coll. Wks. 14*, Para. 117.
4. *Ibid.*, Para. 126.
5. *Ibid.*, p. 97, n. 38.

CHAPTER THREE

1. Cited by Jung, *Coll. Wks. 14*, Para. 251; from Preisendanz, *Pap. Graec. Mag.*, I, pp. 110ff. Pap. IV, 1115-66.
2. Jung, *op. cit.*, Para. 256ff.
3. *Ibid.*, Para. 374.
4. *Ibid.*
5. Joannes C. Steeb, *Coelum sephiroticum Hebraeorum*, Mainz, 1679, pp. 33, 38. Cited in Jung, *Coll. Wks. 11*, p. 98, n. 65.

CHAPTER FOUR

1. Steeb, *op. cit.*
2. Jung, *Coll. Wks. 9, i*, "Archetypes of the Collective Unconscious," Para. 41; *Coll. Wks. 8*, "Analytical Psychology and *Weltanschauung*," Para. 729; "Synchronicity: An Acausal Connecting Principle," Para. 957ff.
3. Steeb, *op. cit.*, p. 38.

CHAPTER FIVE

1. Jung, *Coll. Wks. 14*, Para. 207ff, 523 and n. 402.
2. *Ibid.*, Para. 603.
3. Joannes Lydus, *De. mensibus*, II, 11, ed. Richard Wünsch, Leipzig, 1898. Cited in Jung, *Coll. Wks. 16*, Para. 451, n. 8.

NOTES

4. Hippolytus, *Elenchos*, V, 19, 14ff. Quoted in Jung, *Coll. Wks. 14,* Para. 327.

5. Jung, *Coll. Wks, 14*, Para. 427.

6. Hippolytus, *op. cit.*, V, 16, 8f. Cited in Jung, *ibid.,* n. 691.

7. Brugsch, *Religion und Mythologie der alten Ägypter*, pp. 130ff. Quoted in Jung, *ibid.,* Para. 483.

8. Hippolytus, *op. cit.*, V, 17, 8ff. Quoted in Jung, *Coll. Wks. 9, ii*, Para. 290.

INDEX

dark, 12, 13, 21; darkness visible, 16; recurrence of, 26

"Dark Water," 104, 111, 112, 113, 119, 120, 142, 143, 147, 154-5, 165; canine nature, 112; deeper meaning, 114-6, 137; Persephone's *phlua*, 102, 111; primordial feminine, 82, 104, 137; sacred to Diana, 105; in sympathetic nervous system, 123; union with "Flowing Light," 140

death, 10, 27, 40, 130, 133, 134, 141-2, 150; archetypal, 135, 162-3; realm of, 162-3; state of, 25; waters of, 85

Demiurge, 146

depression, 8, 15, 39, 40, 44, 45, 67

desert, 65, 74, 78, 83, 86

deus terrenus, 153

devil, 28, 31; *see also* Lucifer

Diana, 105, 106, 114

Dionysus, 68, 76, 152

dissolutio, 53, 91

dissolution, 11, 12, 20

divine child, 17

divine *logoi*, 120; as symbols, 117

dog, 101, 103-7, 109, 111, 133, 134; becomes eagle, 106; cat-like, 108; and hydrophobia, 105, 113, 138; male, 78, 88; rabid, 104-7, 154; shadow side of ego, 106-7; transformed, 142

dragon, 27, 76, 88, 100, 104, 107; winged and wingless, 114, 156-7

dry: -dock, 18; -ness, 24; vaporizing, 78

eagle, 27, 88, 107, 154

earth, 17, 18, 19, 20, 26, 49, 80; black sun in, 135; fatty, 80; spirit in, 107

earthquake, 130-1, 133-4, 140, 142, 147, 156

eclipse, 11, 12, 14, 26, 33, 67; analogous to earthquake, 134; at Christ's death, 133; dual, 105

ego, 21, 41, 42, 49, 50, 56, 67, 72, 83, 94, 123, 128, 142; conscious complex, 17, 21; -consciousness, 10, 23; dark center of consciousness, 22; dark body of, 10; dream-, 122-3; -ism, 6, 36, 67; empirical, 89; feminine, 5; identification of, 8; limitation of, 89; as mirror in unconscious, 9; non-, 86; precursor to, 58; and self, 94, 122-3, 141-2, -son, 61; symbolic, 122-3; transformed, 78; unconscious aspect, 10

Elenchos: of Hippolytus, 162

England (English), 46, 47, 65

epileptic (epilepsy), 19, 23, 34; dream of, 18

Erinyes, 103, *see also* Furies

175

poison, 14, 15, 16, 17, 19, 86, 88, 154; -panacea, 87-8, 92, 93, 96

pork, 47, 48, 49, 50, 53, 66, 68, 74, 78, 83, 86, 97, 109, 116, 139

power: -drive, 51; will to -, 56; -instinct, 139

pregnancy, 52, 53, 74, 143; -diet, 53, 139, 151-2; images of, 145; pseudo-, 52

pride, 9, 56, 67

prima materia, 29-30, 35-7, 40, 48, 49, 68, 73-6, 86; blackness of, 81; feminine, 48, 49, 79, 118, 137; germ of unity, 104; of *lapis,* 87, 95; of moral experience, 120; unconscious as, 17, 21, 23, 24, 26, 27, 29

privatio lucis, 26

projection (s), 13, 16, 21, 28, 72, 78; as creation of a world, 107; Mercurius, 109; withdrawal, 69

prudery, 55, 137; *see also pudor*

psyche, 10, 11, 12, 20, 28, 54, 70, 71, 73, 86, 88, 108-9, 121, 165; animal, 23, 90, 119, 153; biological, 83, 103, 137; collective, 42; diurnal, 61; luminaries of, 11; phylogenetic, 111; physiological, 54, 70, 73, 74, 83, 121, 155; poles of, 23; psychoid level, 89-90, 137; subjective level, 63

psychogonia, 118, 144, 165

psychoid: level, 19, 138, 161; paradox, 89, 126; -process, 71, 73, 108-9, 126, 153, 163, 165; processes of nervous system, 22

psychosomatic, 65, 68, 72

puberty, 52, 53

pudor, 54-5, 74, 120, 137, 141

puer, 163

quaternio, 87

quick silver, 19

quinta essentia (quintessence), 20, 22, 72, 87, 159; *see also anima mundi,* fifth

rage, 44, 46, 48 51, 52, 57, 60, 66, 67, 68, 70, 77, 101, 111, 112

raven, 88, 134

rebirth, 11, 12, 20

red, 76, 77, 87; blood, 84; -dress, 75, 78, 83, 97, 112, 116, 134; -ness, 24; tincture, 24; *see also* sulphur, *rubedo*

Red Sea, see sea

regression, 48; liberation, 93; regressive union, 50

remorse, 140-1, 147, 156, 165

resurrection, 40, 130, 133, 141-2

Rhea, 104

rhinoceros, 27

ritual, 35, 36, 138-9

179

RE-ANIMATING THE HEART OF IMAGINATION

Alchemical Active Imagination
MARIE-LOUISE VON FRANZ

Working with the text of Gerhard Dorn, an alchemist and physician of the six-teenth century, von Franz presents alchemy as a therapy of the soul. These six chapters, originally delivered as lectures at the Jung Institute, Zurich, open therapeutic insights into the relations among spirit, soul, and body in the ac-tual practice of imagination. (116 pp.)

The New Gnosis: Heidegger, Hillman, and Angels
ROBERTS AVENS

Gnosis, in the hands of Roberts Avens, is a perennial philosophy of the heart. He provides a readable, uncomplicated, and reliable introduction to the Gnosis going on today in the poetical thought of Martin Heidegger and the archetypal psychology of James Hillman. As a *psychological* philosopher, Avens brings fresh meanings to basic gnostic ideas about angels, salvation through knowl-edge, and the world as alive and ensouled. (155 pp.)

On Poetic Imagination and Reverie: Selections from Gaston Bachelard
COLETTE GAUDIN, TR.

Gaston Bachelard initiated a wholly new method of working with matter—and with method itself. His books on the psychoanalysis of fire and the poetics of air, water, earth, and space—excerpted here—have become indispensable for the study of dreams, poetic images, alchemical symbols, and all forms of re-verie. His prodigious ability has produced the single most important body of thought in the rehabilitation of imagination in this century. An introduction to his work that brilliantly and concisely captures his genius. Bibliography of works by and on Bachelard, with a new preface by Gaudin supplementing her introduction of 1970. (lviii, 112 pp.)

God Is a Trauma: Vicarious Religion and Soul-Making
GREG MOGENSON

By presenting a theology of the soul, rather than of the spirit, Mogenson suc-ceeds in bringing together religion and psychology. A God who legislates against images—the language of the soul—fails to provide a context in which the soul can place its pain. Psychologically, the "no-name" God of mono-theism pushes the psyche into a foreign territory where there is no discrimina-tion, subtlety or complexity. Transcendence into spiritual literalism is only an escape from suffering; it fails to find an individual design in the tapestry of the soul's fate. Though a theology of spirit exposes a person to the sadism of the spirit, a theology of soul could strengthen a person's psychological religion by refining the religious imagination. Spirit and soul can reconcile, in religion, when the soul is given its due. (ca. 160 pp.)

Spring Publications, Inc. • P.O. Box 222069 • Dallas, TX 75222